DEFEATING SATAN

DEFEATING SATAN

A Battle Guide to Spiritual Warfare

Dave G. Becher

Copyright © 2019, Dave G. Becher

All rights reserved. No part of this book may be reproduced, scanned, or distributed in any printed or electronic form without permission.

All Bible quotations are from the Authorized (King James) Version.

First Edition: 2019

ISBN: 978-0-9600203-5-5

Text and Cover Design: www.greatwriting.org

Great Writing Publications
www.greatwriting.org
Taylors, SC, USA

Preface

I came to write this book because I noticed that with the increased assault on religion we've seen over the past few decades, we've also seen a corollary increase in despair, depression, suicides, drug and alcohol abuse, hate crimes, and even school shootings of children by children. We've surrendered our spiritual garrison—the "nation under God" built upon faith—by allowing the assault on religion to continue unabated and generally uncontested. As a result, we are now living in a land under occupied forces. America the religious has become a harlot nation under secularists where abominations abound.

By incrementally yielding the spiritual ground to Satan and his followers during this long war, we are now reaping the horrible consequences of those decisions. Yet, we need to recapture that lost spiritual ground quickly because we are in the endtimes, according to scriptural prophecies. There is nothing foretold that must happen now before Jesus Christ returns in glory. It has all come to pass. The stage is set. The battle lines are drawn. The endgame is upon us. Judgment is imminent.

Unfortunately, most people today have rejected the notion of a higher, unseen Authority. This is due to the incessant ridicule and mockery of religion by unbelievers, coupled with a secular political correctness inflicted upon us that seeks to punish any outward expressions of religion.

"Even so then at this present time also there is a remnant according to the election of grace" (Romans 11:5). I have written this battle guide for that faithful remnant as a source of fortitude to carry us through the daily skirmishes in preparation and anticipation of the final conflict. We must gird ourselves in the war for our souls each day until final relief comes from Heaven. The clarion call to arms is unmistakable. The war for our souls is coming to a dramatic conclusion. Therefore, we must be educated and trained in the militaristic ways of warfare to fight back the enemy's spiritual assault so that we stand victorious with Christ at the end. Having remained loyal to our King, we will be justly and richly rewarded.

All scriptural quotations are taken from the King James Version of the Bible unless otherwise specified. It should be noted also for the sake of clarity that the *italicized* words in scriptural quotes do not imply emphasis, as is usually the case. Instead, the use of italics in the King James Bible is to identify words that have been *added* to the text by the translators to facilitate understanding, as translation from one language to another often finds difficulties finding corollary words or expressions.

*

I gratefully acknowledge the tireless, creative, and professional efforts by Jim Holmes of Great Writing Publications (www.greatwriting.org) for his invaluable assistance in once again bringing my nonprofessional efforts up to professional par in directing this work toward publication.

Introduction

To solve some mathematical problems, it becomes necessary to reduce them to their simplest forms. It is only then that the numbers become manageable, and the equations made more easily understandable and readily solvable.

In life outside the classroom, this same principle applies to most situations. The bottom line of almost all our problems is a *spiritual* one which can be traced all the way back to the beginning rivalry between God and Satan—the age-old battle of good versus evil—when Satan and his minions rebelled against God and were expelled from Heaven. Since then, the devil has wandered the earth in a relentless pursuit to destroy human souls by leading people into his rebellion, and thereby denying God His due glory and praise.

Many psychiatrists, sociologists, and psychologists seek to peel away and explore the many layers of experiences in our lives to discover the "root causes" of why we think and act as we do. They dig deep to understand certain cultural patterns and behaviors of personality. Seeking *spiritual* root causes in all things makes it possible to diagnose and treat societal inter-relational ailments by reducing those problems to their simplest forms as well. At the bottom of all those problems we can always find the devices of Satan at work.

The temptation thrust upon us by the devil to commit sin is an act of constant warfare upon our souls individually and collectively upon societal morality in all aspects, and at all times. There is no demilitarized zone that Satan respects. Everything is fair game to him. Every one of his actions is a hostile act against us either directly, or indirectly.

The key to defeating that assault is to engage in spiritual warfare. To do so, not only must one put on the full armor of God for defense (see Ephesians 6:10-17), but one must also identify and understand the enemy and his tactics, so as to go on the offense and actively engage him in combat to destroy his strongholds within us and recapture lost spiritual territory. Make no mistake about it; the great enemy of humanity *is* Satan, the Adversary.

Unfortunately, too many people do not believe in the existence of Satan. French poet Charles Baudelaire (1821–1867) once keenly observed that "The devil's finest trick is to persuade you that he does not exist." If you don't believe in him, then you're oblivious to his influence, and therein, vulnerable to his attacks. Yet we know from the historical witness of Jesus of Nazareth—through the Gospels that recorded His testimony—that the devil does, indeed, exist.

Having established his existence, it then becomes necessary to understand who he is, and what his methods and motives are. Because it is a matter of spiritual *warfare*, one must become learned in the military strategies and tactics of human warfare, as they are quite similar in many ways. Therefore, many of the principal strategies used in this book will reference modern warfare tactics, as well as those from ancient guides to warfare such as Sun Tzu's *The Art of War*. By understanding the different aspects of warfare, not only can we expose Satan, but we can learn how to neutralize his attacks upon us, and thereby defeat him.

Table of Contents

Part One—The Individual

Chapter One: There *is* a God	11
Chapter Two: There *is* a Devil	20
Chapter Three: Know the Enemy	27
Chapter Four: Know Yourself	41
Chapter Five: Satan's Arsenal	49
Chapter Six: Defend Yourself	66
Chapter Seven: Draw Strength	73
Chapter Eight: Anticipate the Attack	80
Chapter Nine: Detect Deceit	97
Chapter Ten: Identify Satan's Allies	103
Chapter Eleven: Know the Final Outcome	122

Part Two—Society

Chapter Twelve: Love and Marriage	128
Chapter Thirteen: Business and Industry	139
Chapter Fourteen: Interpersonal Relationships	147
Chapter Fifteen: Politics	156
Chapter Sixteen: Conclusion	187
About the Author	191

Part 1: The Individual

1

There *is* a God

Before accepting the reality of *spiritual* warfare, one must first accept the reality of the *Spirit*. Contrary to right reason, "The fool hath said in his heart, *There is* no God" (Psalm 14:1). Since the creation of humanity all cultures and societies have expressed an innate belief in either a higher being (or beings), or in higher planes of consciousness—through monotheism (one God), polytheism (many gods), or transcendental philosophies. Even the primitive Neanderthal left evidence of religious ceremonies dating back to over a vast length of time. The languages of history prove that the idea of God is universal. Therefore—with the exception of those who choose deliberately to deny it—what all humans have universally believed must be assumed to be undeniably and intuitively true—that there is a spiritual world beyond the world of the flesh. There is life after death.

Science (and common sense) dictates that for every effect, there must also be an adequate cause. The creation of the universe necessarily demands the existence of a Creator. It then follows that the concept of a *finite* universe—with a beginning, and inevitably an end—also demands consideration of the *infinite*.

Though many today insist that all life simply evolved on its own, that premise is scientifically unsound. The First Law of Thermodynamics basically states that energy cannot be created or destroyed, only altered. Yet, from absolute nothingness, we see the explosion of new life grown into a dynamic universe. This implies a force outside of the natural laws of our universe. In other words, a *super*natural being, existing outside of time and space, must have called the *natural* universe into existence.

Decades ago, British astrophysicists Stephen Hawking, Roger Penrose, and George Ellis published a paper on their extension of Albert Einstein's Theory of General Relativity, in which they concluded that both time and space did indeed have a finite beginning. Before that, there was precisely nothing. The sudden introduction of space, time, matter, and energy are attributed by many to a "Big Bang" eruption from an initial singularity, resulting in the universe in which we exist today. That universe is, not coincidentally, ordered by natural laws. Even Einstein remarked, "The most incomprehensible thing about the world is that it is at all comprehensible." What is this Singularity that established those laws? There had to be a master Architect of the design, before it could come to fruition.

We read in the Bible: "In the beginning God created the heaven and the earth" (Genesis 1:1). We now have an explanation much more plausible than the one assuming a completely random or accidental-yet-perfect assembly of atoms clearly evident in the myriad complex interrelated and interdependent life forms and systems of the existing universe. In fact, mathematicians have calculated the odds of life arising on its own from non-life—through unintelligent processes (versus intelligent design)—to be so astronomical as to be, essentially, impossible. Notice also that, unlike the cosmogonies (models depicting the creation of the universe) of other ancient civilizations which are always preceded by theogonies (models depicting the creation of the gods); there is no comparable creation story to account for the God of the Israelites because the one true God has existed eternally.

Over the millennia, there have always been certain people who dismissed the Bible as fiction—continuing even up to this day. Yet, it is now an undisputed fact that the Bible is the most accurate ancient historical document ever written and studied. It has withstood the minutest scientific textual analysis possible, as well having been verified repeatedly by archeology over time. In fact, just recently (August 2017) it was reported that archeological excavators in Jerusalem have discovered burned artifacts, which they dated back to 2,600 years ago. That finding now corroborates the biblical account of the burning of Jerusalem recorded in the Old Testament book of Jeremiah; "Now in ... the nineteenth year of Nebuchadrezzar king of Babylon, came Nebuzaradan, captain of the guard .... And burned the house of the LORD, and the king's house; and all the houses of Jerusalem, and all the houses of the great *men*, burned he with fire" (Jeremiah 52:12–13). That event occurred in the Jewish year of 3416, or 588 BC—2607 years before the (2019) publication of this work.

An even more recent finding (January 2018) of a 2,700 year old clay seal written in ancient Hebrew script, confirms two statements in the Bible (2 Kings 23:8; 2 Chronicles 34:8) that there were governors in Jerusalem appointed by the king. "'It supports the Biblical rendering of the existence of a governor of the city in Jerusalem 2,700 years ago," an [Israeli] Antiquities Authority statement quoted excavator Shlomit Weksler-Bdolah as saying.'"[1] Governors of Jerusalem are mentioned twice in the Bible, (see also 2 Chronicles 26:11).

Archeology confirms biblical narratives of the New Testament as well. Another recent finding, published in August of 2018, confirms the historical existence of the town of Cana, where Jesus attended a wedding and performed His first miracle of turning water into wine. Dr. Tom McCollough notes: "The pilgrim texts we have from this period that describe what pilgrims did and saw when they came to Cana of Galilee match very closely what we have exposed as the veneration complex."[2] He also noted that the location of the uncovered town aligns geographically with descriptions documented by first-century Jewish historian, Flavius Josephus (c. AD 37–100).

Other archeological confirmations of biblical accounts include (but are not limited to): the existence of the Hittite Empire (long thought fictional); the Tower of Babel; Israel

---

[1] Reuters, Staff. "Israeli Archaeologists Find 2,700-year-old 'governor of Jerusalem'..." Reuters. January 01, 2018. Accessed January 01, 2018. https://www.reuters.com/article/us-israel-archaeology/israeli-archaeologists-find-2700-year-old-governor-of-jerusalem-seal-impression-idUSKBN1EQ0WH.

[2] Fish, Tom. "BIBLE BOMBSHELL: Archaeologists Unearth Site of Jesus' 'Water into Wine' Miracle." Dailystar.co.uk. August 30, 2018. Accessed August 30, 2018. https://www.dailystar.co.uk/news/world-news/726563/jesus-bible-miracle-site-gospel-of-john-water-wine.

enslaved in Egypt; Israel in Canaan; the discovery of Jacob's well; the Exodus from Egypt; the location of Pharaoh's stables of horses and chariots that pursued Moses and the Israelites; the battle of Jericho; the existence of King David (long thought fictional); the discovery of King David's palaces; the Philistine use of the name of Goliath at the time of the battle with David; Shishak's invasion of Judah; the Moabite rebellion; the burial plaque of King Uzziah; the obelisk relief of Jehu, king of Israel; Hezekiah's Siloam Tunnel inscription; the royal seal of Hezekiah; the siege of Jerusalem during the reign of Hezekiah; a clay seal impression belonging to Nathan-Melech, an official in the court of King Josiah (mentioned in 2 Kings 23:11); the Bethesda pool; the Pool of Siloam; proof of Belshazzar's Babylonian co-regency at the time of Daniel; the discovery of Samson's spring; the discovery of Elisha's spring; the discovery of the site of the city of Derbe (associated with the city of Lystra in Acts); the existence of Lysanius, the tetrarch of Abilene at the time of John the Baptist's ministry; Jewish ossuaries (chests for the bones of the dead) containing ankle bones with iron nails protruding through them—proving the method of crucifixion by nailing; the discovery in the 1960s of the Pilate Stone and a ring—proving the existence of Pontius Pilate as a Roman governor in the time of Jesus; the November 1990 discovery of an ossuary with the bones of Joseph Caiaphas—high priest over the Sanhedrin trial of Jesus. We've also seen, as well, fulfillment in the historical record of Daniel's prophecies regarding Nebuchadnezzar, the Medo-Persian Empire, Alexander the Great, and the Roman Empire.

> [P]laces such as Haran, Hazor, Dan, Megiddo, Shechem, Samaria, Shiloh, Gezer, Gibeah, Beth Shemesh, Beth Shean, Beersheba, Lachish, and many other urban sites have been excavated, quite apart from such larger and obvious locations as Jerusalem or Babylon. Such geographical markers are extremely significant in demonstrating that *fact*, not *fantasy*, is intended in the Old Testament historical narratives; otherwise, the specificity regarding these urban sites would have been replaced by

"Once upon a time" narratives with only hazy geographical parameters, if any.[3]

At a time when the wisdom of the world was that the earth was flat, the Bible clearly identified the earth as round; "*It is* he that sitteth upon the circle of the earth, and the inhabitants thereof *are* as grasshoppers; that stretcheth out the heavens as a curtain, and spreadeth them out as a tent to dwell in" (Isaiah 40:22). Note, also, that the archeological record has never actually refuted any historical account in the Bible, but only confirmed it.

The science of geology also confirms the biblical accounts of the Flood; the destruction of Sodom and Gomorrah; the damming of the waters of the Jordan River to enable the Israelite crossing; and the earthquake that occurred at the crucifixion, to name a few.

Additional corroboration of the veracity of the Bible's historical value can be found in the fact that every civilization in the world's history has had a flood story correlating with the biblical event of Noah's flood. Josephus, in his *Antiquities of the Jews* (1.3.6), states that "all the writers of barbarian histories make mention of this flood and of this ark."[4] Many of those original written barbarian histories are now lost forever, but their record lives on—having been passed on down to us through subsequent historians over time. Furthermore:

> A recently released study conducted by Mark Steckle and David Thaler, research scientists at the University of Basel, Switzerland, asserts an interesting and unintended Noahic allusion. The study surveyed the mitochondrial DNA of five million animals and 100,000 species and concluded that 99% of all current animal life, including humans, all descended from a single pair of ancestors no

---

[3] "Biblical Archaeology: Factual Evidence to Support the Historicity of the Bible." Christian Research Institute. Accessed January 21, 2018. http://www.equip.org/article/biblical-archaeology-factual-evidence-to-support-the-historicity-of-the-bible/.

[4] Josephus, Flavius. The Works of Josephus: Complete and Unabridged in One Volume. Peabody, Mass: Hendrickson Publishers, 1987. NEW UPDATED EDITION. Translated by William Whiston, A. M.

more than 250,000 years ago following some unknown worldwide cataclysmic event. ... [Darwinian evolutionist] Thaler noted that "this conclusion is very surprising and I fought against it as hard as I could." ... [I]sn't it interesting that the Biblical story of a worldwide flood and pairs of animals saved from the destruction finds scientific support? It's almost as if the Author knew what he was talking about...[5]

Also, the account of Joshua's "long day" in which the sun stood still, seems to be verified in global accounts throughout numerous civilizations of either long days, or of long nights in civilizations on the other side of the globe, recorded as occurring in the same historical timeframe, c. 1400 BC.

Nature also testifies to God's existence; "The heavens declare the glory of God; and the firmament sheweth his handywork. Day unto day uttereth speech, and night unto night sheweth knowledge. *There is* no speech nor language, *where* their voice is not heard" (Psalm 19:1-3). American biblical scholar Dr. Joseph Addison Alexander (1809-1860) wrote of the perpetual testimony "conveyed by the figure of one day and night following another as witnesses in unbroken succession."[6] If there is an intelligent design in the universe, then there must also be an Intelligent Designer. If the lesser works of human creation such as clocks, engines, or buildings—which cannot randomly form and then come together by themselves—also require a creator, how much more so for the vast intricacies of the natural universe and prodigious complexities of life?

Moreover, though the expansive cosmos testifies to a Creator, His designs are observable in everything else—right down to the atomic level. "Advances in molecular biology have revealed vast amounts of information encoded in each and every living cell, and molecular biologists have discovered thousands upon thousands of exquisitely designed machines at the molecular

---

5 "Study Finds Humans Came From One Pair." The Patriot Post. Accessed December 04, 2018. https://patriotpost.us/articles/59803-study-finds-humans-came-from-one-pair.

6 Joseph Addison Alexander, *The Psalms Translated and Explained*, 1864 Edinburgh, p.88

level. Information requires intelligence and design requires a designer."[7] The Great Designer is made manifest through all our studies of science.

The Human Genome Project mapped the entire human genetic code. In a press conference in 2000, U.S. President Bill Clinton remarked: "Today, we are learning the language in which God created life. We are gaining ever more awe for the complexity, the beauty, the wonder of God's most divine and sacred gift." As of this writing, our most intricately designed computer technology still pales in comparison to the immense complexity of divine design. Dr. Joseph Paturi comments on the intricacies of the human body: "Man-made machines are lubricated only by outside sources. But the body lubricates itself by manufacturing a jelly-like substance in the right amount at every place it is needed."[8] Furthermore, Dr. Paturi observes "The body has a chemical plant far more intricate than any plant that man has ever built. This plant changes the food we eat into living tissue. It causes the growth of flesh, blood, bones and teeth. It even repairs the body when parts are damaged by accident or disease." He logically concludes that "The raw material, the basic chemicals in our body, can be found in the 'dust of the ground' [Genesis 2:7]. However, these chemicals cannot arrange themselves into cell tissues, organs and systems. This can only happen with an input of intelligence." As American poet Joyce Kilmer (1886–1918) wrote "Poems are made by fools like me, But only God can make a tree." Despite all of our scientific breakthroughs in understanding life and the universe, we will never be able to create from scratch even a single blade of living grass.

Finally, and most importantly, the historical figure Jesus of Nazareth has also testified to the existence of our Father in Heaven through His firsthand, eyewitness account: "No man hath seen God at any time; the only begotten Son, which is in the bosom of the Father, he hath declared *him*" (John 1:18). Because the finite cannot testify to the infinite, we have personal testimony

---

7 "Does God Exist?" AllAboutPhilosophy.org. 2002. Accessed September 27, 2017. https://www.allaboutphilosophy.org/does-god-exist-c.htm.

8 Paturi, Joseph. "The Human Body-God's Masterpiece." Answers in Genesis. September 1, 1998. Accessed February 23, 2019. https://answersingenesis.org/kids/anatomy/the-human-body/.

from the only One who possesses the most perfect knowledge of God—having resided with Him from *everlasting to everlasting*.

Speaking of Himself in the third person, Jesus further stated: "And no man hath ascended up to heaven, but he that came down from heaven, *even* the Son of man which is in heaven" (John 3:13). He brought the very highest revelation of the one true God down to us through His incarnation, and testified that He was sent by God to this earth: "And this is life eternal, that they might know thee the only true God, and Jesus Christ, whom thou hast sent" (John 17:3). Jesus specifically confirmed to Peter, in front of the other apostles, that there is a God in heaven; "And Jesus answered and said unto him, Blessed art thou, Simon Bar-jona: for flesh and blood hath not revealed *it* unto thee, but my Father which is in heaven" (Matthew 16:17). God had inscribed the truth into Peter's heart to testify that Jesus Christ is "the Son of the living God" (Matthew 16:16). None but the Father could have revealed the Son to him.

Jesus Christ is the single most influential and famous person in the history of the world. Why is that? Consider that when He started out on His redemptive mission from God, He was only a poor carpenter with no worldly status. He had only a dozen initial followers—most of them simple fishermen. He only preached for three and a half years before being violently set upon by the ruling powers of both the Romans and Jewish elders, and put to a horrible, humiliating death at the age of thirty-three. Yet, during those few years, "The blind receive their sight, and the lame walk, the lepers are cleansed, and the deaf hear, the dead are raised up, and the poor have the gospel preached to them" (Matthew 11:5). As a result, He was followed around by multitudes everywhere He went. In fact, once when He desired to be alone, He "... went into the borders of Tyre and Sidon, and entered into an house, and would have no man know *it*: but he could not be hid" (Mark 7:24). His teachings and miracles eventually brought even the mighty Roman Empire to its knees in worship under the Emperor Constantine (c. AD 313), despite Rome's vicious expunging of early Christians. Jesus Christ has the largest religious following in the world today with Christians numbering over two billion people. Again, this is despite the brutal persecutions of early Christians by the Romans and the Jewish elders who were both determined to eradicate the memory of Jesus Christ and His followers completely. In fact, world history is delineated into time before Christ became incarnate, and time after His birth. How could any of this be possible if He were not truly the Son of God? Therefore, His testimony is true. There *is* a God. The cumulative evidence is so overwhelming that those who choose not to believe will be left without excuse upon the final judgment.

2

There *is* a Devil

But what of Satan? Is *he* real, or a myth? Does he simply represent as some suggest, the baser lusts and desires of carnality—an *abstract* principle of evil embodying the brute tendencies toward survival and self-gratification at any cost, devoid of morality—and therefore is not an actual conscious entity?

To accept that view, one must ignore the fact that man was created *without* an inherent evil nature. It was not until Satan (as evil-incarnate) introduced himself in the Garden of Eden, that Eve first imbibed his lies, then ingested the fruit—falling into sin and separation from God. Before succumbing to that temptation, however, humanity was blameless. Therefore, Satan must be a separate, distinct entity who came from *without*, to introduce the nature of rebellion to humans *within*. Furthermore, we see that God first condemned the *serpent* for his seduction of humanity:

> And the LORD God said unto the serpent, Because thou hast done this, thou *art* cursed above all cattle, and above every beast of the field; upon thy belly shalt thou go, and dust shalt thou eat all the days of thy life"
> (Genesis, 3:14).

"Moral responsibility cannot be attributed to an abstract principle of evil, only to an intelligent creature capable of both moral and immoral conduct."[9] There would be no condemnation of the serpent if the fault originated solely within Adam and Eve. The

---

9 "The Personality of the Devil." Connection and Perception -- The Five Senses. Accessed 10/1/17. http://www.heraldmag.org/bookstore/booklet_devil.htm.

serpent therefore was the agent of evil who sabotaged the peace between God and humanity.

The literal translation of Satan is *Adversary*. The chief entity we know as Satan was originally an Archangel created by God who may actually have been the highest-ranking angel in heaven. Satan is also known by many as Lucifer. The name of Lucifer however is mentioned only once in the King James Version of the Bible. It has been removed completely from many other later translations. It is a Latin translation meaning "morning star" of the Hebrew word *Hêlêl* for "shining one" or *Helel ben Shachar*, "shining one, son of the morning." It is only found in Isaiah 14:12 "How art thou fallen from heaven, O Lucifer, son of the morning! *how* art thou cut down to the ground, which didst weaken the nations!" The verse in Isaiah was originally referring to a fallen Babylonian king who once ruled the Middle Eastern world. There is much debate as to whether or not the verses are metaphorical depictions of Satan as well. If so, then Lucifer is the name of the original angel just as God created him, nearly perfect, who became filled with pride in himself—thereby *creating* sin—and rebelled against God by exalting himself instead. "And he said unto them, I beheld Satan as lightning fall from heaven" (Luke 10:18). He was expelled from heaven for being adversarial to God's glory, and became known thereafter as Satan.

John 8:44 states that: "He was a murderer from the beginning, and abode not in the truth, because there is no truth in him. When he speaketh a lie, he speaketh of his own: for he is a liar, and the father of it." Since Lucifer was once favored by God, then this verse can only refer to Lucifer after his fall from grace, when he tempted Eve and Adam to sin, thereby making him a murderer "from the beginning" of *human* existence, knowing that they would forfeit their immortality through disobedience to God and thereby impute their "original sin" to all of subsequent humanity resulting in lives of toil, pain, and death.

In his rebellion, he convinced one third of the angels to follow him. This likely occurred sometime after the formation of the earth, but before the creation of man, for when God challenged Job (38:6–7) He asked "... who laid the corner stone thereof; When the morning stars sang together, and all the sons of God shouted

21

for joy?" The only "sons of God" existing during the creation of the universe were the angels. The reference to *all* of them, therefore, must include the pre-rebellious ones as well.

We know of the consequences after the rebellion in heaven; "And the great dragon was cast out, that old serpent, called the Devil, and Satan, which deceiveth the whole world: he was cast out into the earth, and his angels were cast out with him" (Revelation 12:9). The defiant followers of the devil forfeited their exalted titles of *angel*, and hereafter became referred to in Scripture as *demons*. Though the apocryphal Book of Enoch (1 Enoch 69:4-12—referred to in Jude) speaks of five satans (adversaries), the chief ringleader in sin at the top of the command structure— the prince of the demons—shall be the enemy identified in this work as Satan. He is the superior spirit in the hierarchy of demons occupying the top position in the chain of command. He is the enemy supreme commander we need to conquer.

"TaNaK, or Tanakh, is an acronym for the Hebrew Bible consisting of the initial Hebrew letters (T + N + K) of each of the text's three major parts."[10] The Tanak pairs the name of Satan with the definite article *ha* (the) as HaSatan, meaning, *The Satan*, (translated as *The Adversary*), indicating that it should be considered as a proper name for the embodiment of evil—the one who challenged God. He is specifically referenced throughout Scripture as the devil—not *a* devil, but *the* devil. All references to Satan (HaSatan, Beelzebub, Belial, Baal, Serpent, Dragon, Enemy, Tempter, Accuser, etc.) are always in the singular. Jesus cast out many *demons* and *unclean spirits* (plural) throughout His ministry. Yet, when He was targeted by the prince of this world— the devil himself (in an attempt to get Jesus to bow down before him in the wilderness before commencing His ministry)—Jesus specifically called him out by the name of Satan, as we read in Matthew 4:10-11: "Then saith Jesus unto him, Get thee hence, Satan: for it is written, Thou shalt worship the Lord thy God, and him only shalt thou serve. Then the devil leaveth him, and, behold, angels came and ministered unto him." Jesus definitively identified the chief adversary in this world who wars against the

---

10 "TaNaK." Ohio River - New World Encyclopedia. Accessed October 01, 2017. http://www.newworldencyclopedia.org/entry/TaNaK.

Spirit of God as Satan, and rebuked him.

We see Satan again called out by name when Peter (under the influence of the devil) attempted to dissuade Jesus to forsake the work of man's redemption and salvation: "But he turned, and said unto Peter, Get thee behind me, Satan: thou art an offence unto me: for thou savourest not the things that be of God, but those that be of men" (Matthew 16:23). Jesus once again clearly identified and exposed the same adversary as before.

And we see the Lord God rebuking Satan by name: "And he shewed me Joshua the high priest standing before the angel of the LORD, and Satan standing at his right hand to resist him. And the LORD said unto Satan, The LORD rebuke thee, O Satan .... (Zechariah 3:1–2). Clearly Satan exists and is referred to as a singular entity.

These three examples of God and Jesus putting the devil to flight—by simple spoken rebuke—make plain one fact for certain: Satan is subservient to both the Father and the Son. This is a reassuring proof to us that there are limits to Satan's mastery—that he is not all-powerful as God is—and can therefore be defeated because he cannot *force* us to sin, but only *entice* us to do so. Temptation is his chief weapon. Therefore, the choice to sin or not to sin at a critical point (the go/no-go decision) lies solely within us to make.

We see further proof of his subservience in the Old Testament, when Satan desired to test Job's allegiance to God. Note that before Satan could attempt to provoke Job to sin, he first had to request permission of God to proceed with his plan. In answer: "And the LORD said unto Satan, Behold, all that he hath *is* in thy power; only upon himself put not forth thine hand. So Satan went forth from the presence of the LORD" (Job 1:12). God placed limitations on Satan's trials of Job just as He does for us today. We will not be tempted beyond what we can bear—see 1 Corinthians 10:13.

Jesus mentions another incident, one in which Satan had requested to test Peter. "And the Lord said, Simon, Simon, behold, Satan hath desired *to have* you, that he may sift *you* as wheat" (Luke 22:31). Again, we see that Satan must request permission first, before assaulting the people of God.

There are further examples in Scripture of the devil being acknowledged by name. In having his plans to spread the gospel obstructed, Paul wrote: "Wherefore we would have come unto you, even I Paul, once and again; but Satan hindered us (1 Thessalonians 2:18)." Also, we read of Satan's successful plot in 1 Chronicles 21:1; "And Satan stood up against Israel, and provoked David to number Israel." His evil deeds of temptation are recorded for our benefit as proof of his existence and as a warning to be wary of his guile.

What do we know of Satan's appearance? Contrary to popular opinion of a devil with horns in a red suit and pitchfork, Satan was radiantly beautiful in the beginning. It was his beauty that germinated the pride to worship himself, which fomented his rebellion against God. Many scholars and commentaries agree that the verses in Ezekiel which describe the king of Tyre actually have a double-meaning to include a description of Satan. We read in Ezekiel 28:12–17:

> ...Thou sealest up the sum, full of wisdom, and perfect in beauty. Thou hast been in Eden the garden of God; every precious stone *was* thy covering, the sardius, topaz, and the diamond, the beryl, the onyx, and the jasper, the sapphire, the emerald, and the carbuncle, and gold: the workmanship of thy tabrets and of thy pipes was prepared in thee in the day that thou wast created. Thou *art* the anointed cherub that covereth; and I have set thee *so*: thou wast upon the holy mountain of God; thou hast walked up and down in the midst of the stones of fire. Thou *wast* perfect in thy ways from the day that thou wast created, till iniquity was found in thee. By the multitude of thy merchandise they have filled the midst of thee with violence, and thou hast sinned: therefore I will cast thee as profane out of the mountain of God: and I will destroy thee, O covering cherub, from the midst of the stones of fire. Thine heart was lifted up because of thy beauty, thou hast corrupted thy wisdom by reason of thy brightness: I will cast thee to the ground ....

This description as "being in the Garden of Eden ... anointed cherub ... upon the holy mountain of God" cannot literally be applied to any earthly king and therefore must be metaphorically referring to someone else.

In summary, we know that Satan is a real person. He was *created* by God, therefore he cannot be *equal* to God, and, so, has limited power. He was an Archangel who succumbed to personal pride and was thrown out of heaven. We also know that he commands the army of his fellow fallen angels. He roams the earth seeking souls to destroy. As part of his growing army, he also commands an increasing number of human disbelievers through "... the spirit that now worketh in the children of disobedience" (Ephesians 2:2) which he often employs as ancillary reserve troops to attack God's faithful. He was once beautiful, but is now ugly as evil incarnate. Yet, he can still appear radiant through deception, as St. Paul warns us: "And no marvel; for Satan himself is transformed into an angel of light" (2 Corinthians 11:14). He is a liar and a murderer. Knowing all these things about him should keep us on our constant guard in readiness for his attacks.

In *The Art of War* (ch.I, ss.13), Chinese general and military strategist Sun Tzu (544–496 BC) advises that before engaging in battle, one must determine the superiority of forces. To do so, one must first ascertain which of the two sovereigns (in this case the God of heaven versus the god of this world) is imbued with the Moral Law; which of the two generals (Christ or Satan) has most ability; and which army is stronger. The answer to all three is found in the forces of heaven.

- It was God who made the universe. "And God saw every thing that he had made, and, behold, *it was* very good" (Genesis 1:31), "and all the sons of God shouted for joy" (Job 38:7). Satan was the one who rebelled against his Creator, thereby throwing off the Moral Law.
- We've already seen examples of Christ's dominion over Satan. The Gospels are filled with examples of Christ's dominion over every other aspect of creation as well. There is *no* indication of Satan ever being able to control the winds and seas, or exhibiting power over life

and death, as we see repeatedly occurring through the power of Jesus relayed to us through the four separate Gospel accounts. Clearly, Christ is the stronger general through unlimited ability.
- We know that Satan lured one third of the angels away with him in rebellion. That then leaves a two-thirds superior force of loyal angels in heaven. Choosing to fight on the side of God against Satan is obviously the most moral and militarily-sound choice according to ancient military wisdom.

3

Know the Enemy

Our fight against Satan can be described as an example of asymmetric warfare, in which the two combatants are unevenly matched. Satan was created as an Archangel, and has dwelt within the presence of God. Though he is fallen from heaven, he is temporarily "the god of this world" (2 Corinthians 4:4) with legions of demons at his command. We, on the other hand, often stand alone as weak, mortal humans—dependent entirely upon our wavering faith. Sun Tzu taught that "He who exercises no forethought but makes light of his opponent is sure to be captured by them" (ch.IX, ss.41). Fortunately for us, asymmetric warfare does not guarantee victory to the more powerful force. The weaker often prevail by the use of superior strategy, secret weapons, and/or the assistance of powerful allies. Our superior strategy is found in our battlefield manual contained in Scripture; our secret weapon is prayer; our all-powerful ally is Jesus Christ.

To defeat an enemy, it is first necessary to *know* the enemy. We must discover his personal character as well as learning his tactics, strategies, and preferred weapons of warfare. As observed previously in this book (Chapter Two), we know that Satan is a liar, a deceiver, and a murderer. His enemy is all of humanity—even those who think they serve him. We know from Job 1:7 that he is restless in his pursuit of souls: "And the LORD said unto Satan, Whence comest thou? Then Satan answered the LORD, and said, From going to and fro in the earth, and from walking up and down in it." And we know that his intention in pursuing souls is to destroy them "... because your adversary the devil, as a roaring lion, walketh about, seeking whom he may devour" (1 Peter 5:8).

It is all important, then, to understand that his intentions toward us stem from pure malice and therefore should never be ignored, dismissed, or entertained. Satan observes absolutely no limiting Rules of Engagement in his assaults.

Next, we need to identify his tactics. Insight into his strategies will give us an advantage. Because the devil is "the father of lies" and master of deception, this gives him an enormous military advantage. Concealing true intentions in any endeavor to ambush is paramount to victory. Satan's spiritual ambush relies foremost upon our doubt in his existence, so that from a position of concealment, he can then create doubt in us as to the existence of God and thereby deprive us of any alliance with Him. Unfortunately, this effort is aided and abetted by many influential people—including authors, actors, producers, professors, politicians, and journalists. "Is God dead?" was the cover of a 1966 issue of *Time Magazine*.

Dan Brown, author of *The DaVinci Code* series of books, expresses the "new-age" way of thinking: "We will start to find our spiritual experiences through our interconnections with each other ... [and through the emergence of] ... some form of global consciousness that we perceive and that becomes our divine. ... Our need for that exterior god, that sits up there and judges us ... will diminish and eventually disappear."[11] If we don't believe we need a personal God, or if we believe that He is just an impersonal force, then we can never enjoy an intimate personal relationship with Him and we are then effectively cut off from communicating with our greatest ally.

Furthermore, if we don't believe that God exists at all, then we cannot believe in Jesus Christ, His Son. If we do not believe that Jesus Christ is the Son of the living God who was sent to pay the sin debt for humanity, we cannot be washed clean of our sins, and we will be denied entry into heaven. And so the road to perdition is a slippery slope iced over with exactly this type of "enlightened" thinking. That is Satan's military objective in this deception—making the retrogressive sound progressive. We can see this strategy carried out in numerous ways if we but look

---

11 Busvine, Douglas, "Collective consciousness to replace God – author Dan Brown," Reuters, accessed October 12, 2017, https://www.yahoo.com/news/collective-consciousness-replace-god-author-dan-brown-120033225.html

through the discerning, surveilling eye of scriptural scrutiny.

One great foothold Satan gains against God and religion is through the courts and legal systems. In the days when the apostles preached, the Jewish rulers, elders, and scribes outlawed their doctrine; "And they called them, and commanded them not to speak at all nor teach in the name of Jesus" (Acts 4:18). We see this policy continued to date under the phony guise of "separation of church and state." Contrary to popular opinion, there is absolutely *nothing* in the U.S. Constitution which justifies the governmental assault against religion we've been witness to since prayer in school was first abolished over fifty years ago in this country. The Constitution's *Establishment Clause* does state that "Congress shall make no law respecting an establishment of religion ...." In other words, it prohibits establishing a national religion, such as The Church of America, modeling, say, The Church of England established by King Henry VIII. But the second half of that clause is always neglected: "... or prohibiting the free exercise thereof." In America, people are free to worship when, and where, they see fit. Therefore, the "separation of church and state" doctrine is abused through a tortured interpretation and becomes, instead, a doctrine advocating for the separation of the church and people—*by* the state. The original intent of the Supreme Court ruling was to end *mandatory* prayer in school to give exemptions to those who did not believe, but it has instead become the catchall to prohibit even *voluntary* prayer if it occurs in any public building, or on public grounds. As a result of removing this early bulwark against deviancy in the lives of our children, we see now that instead of prayer in school, we have security guards in school with metal detectors seeking guns and knives to thwart gang violence and mass murder. Is it any wonder that we are also seeing a rise in Satanism in this country as well as a commensurate rise in the demand for exorcisms? In 2011, the U.S. had about fifteen Catholic exorcists. Because of the recent demand due to the rise in reported demonic possessions, we now have over one hundred.[12]

Extension of this all-out assault on religion into every other

---

12 Mariani, Mike. "American Exorcism." The Atlantic. November 20, 2018. Accessed November 28, 2018. https://www.theatlantic.com/magazine/archive/2018/12/catholic-exorcisms-on-the-rise/573943/.

public venue has resulted in the Ten Commandment plaques that adorn courthouses across the nation—reminders that we received our moral law from God—being taken down through successful lawsuit adjudication filed by atheists, and abetted by a religious-hostile judiciary. A federal judge decreed, as recently as October 2017, in favor of a group of atheists, that the "Peace Cross" fallen-soldier memorial, erected in 1925 by the American Legion in Bladensburg, Maryland, must be torn down.[13] (A 7-2 Supreme Court ruling in June of 2019 reversed that decision.)

The Plaintiff in the case, the American Humanist Association, believes in "being good without a god." This is impossible. "And Jesus said unto him, Why callest thou me good? none *is* good, save one, *that is*, God" (Luke 18:19). Scripture clearly states: "But we are all as an unclean *thing*, and all our righteousnesses *are* as filthy rags; and we all do fade as a leaf; and our iniquities, like the wind, have taken us away" (Isaiah 64:6). Without the cleansing of our sins by a holy and gracious God through Christ's sacrifice on the cross, our sin remains, so that "As it is written, There is none righteous, no, not one" (Romans 3:10). We also now have abortion on demand as the law of the land forced upon us through a usurping judicial fiat, because the will of the people—decided through elections and legislation—would never have allowed it to become a national policy. This horrible infanticide includes murdering babies, even as they are being born, in a gruesome procedure known as partial-birth abortion.

Not only is any expression of religion becoming banned in public, but people are being vigorously prosecuted for any violation of those misinterpreted laws. The persecution campaign against religion extends even down to very young children in school saying grace over their lunch before eating it—as they were properly raised to do. Unbelievably, there *are* recorded instances of children being sent to detention for committing that "crime," as well as for saying "God bless you" to a sneezing classmate, and for bringing a Bible to school and sharing it with others. In its place, a godless secular agenda is being promoted.

---

13 Bradford Richardson, "Peace Cross of Bladensburg ruled unconstitutional by appeals court" accessed October 21, 2017, http://www.washingtontimes.com/news/2017/oct/18/peace-cross-of-bladensburg-ruled-unconstitutional-/

The Bible has been banned, but condoms are now handed out freely and "safe sex" preached to children instead. Florida State Senator, Steve Oehlrich, correctly laments: "You can't give a child an aspirin in school without permission. You can't do any kind of medication, but we can secretly take the child off and have an abortion."[14] When challenged on this statement, Politifact Florida investigated it and rated his claim as true.

With the end times upon us, Satan has intensified his war on society. His blitzkrieg against western civilization in the 1960s through the hippie countercultural movement, attained great success. In a few short decades, he has greatly unraveled the moral fabric of our society. Political journalist Brian Mark Weber observes some of the results:

> This is what the '60s counterculture has given us. Traditional marriage is oppressive and discriminatory. Porn is ever present, even among our children. Men are welcomed into women's bathrooms (and one has been charged with raping a 10-year-old). Gender is subjective. *Heather has Two Mommies* is actually the title of a children's book, and a drag queen "demon" reads books to children at school. Even pedophilia is normalized.[15]

Not content with outlawing the free public expression of religion, the tactic is taken even further to mock and ridicule the religious as being backward and dangerous people, going so far as to attribute a motive of "hate" to their actions and speech. Preaching the gospel is now considered to be—by many of the so-called *enlightened*—a "hate crime" because it condemns the sinful lifestyles of those self-proclaimed *enlightened*—lifestyles which God has irreversibly decreed in Scripture as "abominable." Many Jewish and Christian organizations, churches, and synagogues are themselves being condemned as "hate groups" by

---

14 Sanders, Katie. "State Senator Claims School Nurses Can't Give Aspirin without Parent's Permission." @politifact. May 17, 2011. Accessed December 06, 2018. https://www.politifact.com/florida/statements/2011/may/17/steve-oelrich/state-senator-claims-school-nurses-cant-give-aspir/.

15 Brian Mark Weber, "Hollywood Outraged at the Monster it Created," accessed October 20, 2017, https://patriotpost.us/articles/51965

radical agents of the devil. There was an actual debate on campus at Kent State University in October of 2017, over whether telling someone "You need Jesus" constituted hate speech.[16]

On July 30, 2018, U.S. Attorney General Jeff Sessions delivered remarks at the Department of Justice's Religious Liberty Summit. In those remarks he acknowledged this anti-religion trend:

> A dangerous movement, undetected by many, is now challenging and eroding our great tradition of religious freedom. There can be no doubt. This is no little matter. It must be confronted and defeated. ...We have gotten to the point where courts have held that morality cannot be a basis for law; where ministers are fearful to affirm, as they understand it, holy writ from the pulpit; and where one group can actively target religious groups by labeling them a "hate group" on the basis of their sincerely held religious beliefs.[17]

Fortunately, those comments were followed up by Sessions with a declaration that the Trump administration has created the Religious Liberty Task Force to defend religious liberty in America and address those concerns.

The invention of "Political Correctness" was a way to inoculate Satan's advocates against any sort of criticism of their ungodly ways, while forcing submission to, and acceptance of, their ungodly principles under threat of ostracization. People's lives and careers have been ruined for being politically *incorrect* in speaking out against any of a number of Satan's favorite groups. That stigmatization is promulgated through Satan's alliance with secular mainstream media outlets so that the intolerance of religion becomes a widespread phenomenon within a manipulated public, resulting in the total banishment from the public arena

---

16 Colin Cortbus, "Kent State mulls whether telling someone 'You need Jesus' is hate speech," accessed October 25, 2017, https://www.thecollegefix.com/post/38242/

17 "Attorney General Sessions Delivers Remarks at the Department of Justice's Religious Liberty Summit." The United States Department of Justice. Accessed July 31, 2018. https://www.justice.gov/opa/speech/attorney-general-sessions-delivers-remarks-department-justice-s-religious-liberty-summit.

we see playing out through the courts today. "[T]he god of this world hath blinded the minds of them which believe not, lest the light of the glorious gospel of Christ, who is the image of God, should shine unto them" (2 Corinthians 4:4). Satan cannot allow the message of heaven to be disseminated, lest it resonate and thereby lead people to salvation. Those he has enslaved he intends to keep imprisoned through gospel ignorance. He then employs those "useful idiots" (Vladimir Lenin's term) to do likewise unto others—recruit through ignorance.

Another method Satan uses to silence opposing viewpoints is through the widespread employment of epithets. Name-calling is the easiest and quickest method of communicating a negative view of a person or group without actually engaging in honest debate with that person or group. Negatively label people, and it automatically serves to disqualify their viewpoint from consideration. It has the added bonus that it can be applied almost universally to any opposing group of individuals. Calling a person a racist divides people along the lines of racial or cultural backgrounds and shuts down any meaningful dialogue on obtaining racial harmony. Labeling someone a sexist drives a wedge between men and women, etc.

Pitting one group of people against another is the ultimate goal—to sow discord, whether through the shallow criteria of being fat or thin, tall or short; or through fostering more deep-seated prejudices of religious belief as found in the long-standing animosity between Muslims and Jews, the end result is the same—sowing division and strife to inculcate fear, suspicion, and hatred. Success of this tactic is demonstrated in a recent poll taken by NPR, the Robert Wood Johnson Foundation, and the Harvard T. H. Chan School of Public Health, which found majorities in all groups of people believing that they are discriminated against.[18] Victimizing entire groups of people necessarily creates those enemies (real or imagined) who would perpetrate bias against them, resulting in class warfare on all levels.

---

18 Joe Neel, "Poll: Most Americans Think Their Own Group Faces Discrimination, accessed November 1, 2017, http://www.npr.org/sections/health-shots/2017/10/24/559116373/poll-most-americans-think-their-own-group-faces-discrimination

Another tactic in Satan's battle plan is the use of distraction. After sowing seeds of division through mistrust and fear of one another, he uses those gains to divide us even further through enabling wars, crime, civil unrest, and disobedience. All these distractions are akin to the magician's misdirection, so that Satan's manipulation is screened from detection. Suddenly, our lives become full of fear and anxiety, thereby robbing us of our God-given inner peace—all the while the chief agitator stealthily gains spiritual ground against us.

Other distractions are presented as fascinations, which eventually become false idols. Obsessions with money, sex, social media, cell phones, technology, etc., become all-consuming so that "... the cares of this world, and the deceitfulness of riches, and the lusts of other things entering in, choke the word, and it becometh unfruitful" (Mark 4:19). In fact, people are so distracted by their electronic devices today that we consistently read in the news of people dying while trying to retrieve dropped cell phones from under buses or on train tracks, or of one person even falling off a cliff texting while hiking.

Imagine the disappointment of an angel of God being sent down to earth for the first time to observe humanity at this crucial point in time. At first glance upon his descent, he might marvel at how holy the world is, seeing everyone walking around with heads bowed and hands folded in thoughtful prayer. As he got closer, though, he would sadly realize that hardly anyone is praying at all. They are all simply staring into their hands and playing with their cell phones as they worship at the altar of technology with every free moment they have—and all the while Satan laughs maniacally at the success of his deception objective.

Another key element to military victory is obtained through secret infiltration of the enemy's defenses. Spies have been mentioned numerous times in the Old Testament, dating back thousands of years. Sun Tzu listed five classes of spies in his ancient treatise on war. In *ch.*XIII, *ss.*18, he emphasizes the need for subtlety, and to use spies "for every kind of business." Though spies in general are employed to obtain secret information, Satan's spies are propagandists used to disseminate his secret agenda to deflect attention away from God and morality. He has infiltrated every institution under the guise of "tolerance" and "inclusion" to destroy the notion of sin and immorality.

He is especially active in the church. He was there right at the founding of the early Christian church when he seduced Ananias and Sapphira to lie about their generosity. Thankfully, their deceit did not go undetected; "But Peter said, Ananias, why hath Satan filled thine heart to lie to the Holy Ghost, and to keep back *part* of the price of the land?" (Acts 5:3). Though thwarted then, he's been much more successful since. The latest Barna Research on the condition of churches in the United States reveals that eight out of ten churches surveyed "did not read the Bible and did not feature a message centered on Scripture."[19] Barna (in partnership with Seed Company) also discovered in a 2018 survey that more than half of churchgoers surveyed had not even heard of the "Great Commission."[20]

The Great Commission was commanded by Jesus of all Christians, to "Go ye therefore, and teach all nations, baptizing them in the name of the Father, and of the Son, and of the Holy Ghost: Teaching them to observe all things whatsoever I have commanded you" (Matthew 28:19–20). By diverting attention away from this mandate, Satan thwarts the ministry of the gospel and thereby hinders the spread of Christianity throughout the world, leaving people to wander lost in the wilderness of worldliness. He then captures those distressed persons who were not able to evade him because they were never taught biblical map reading or spiritual navigation skills to discover the path to salvation through Christ.

Unable to *completely* silence the message, Satan is very active in perverting the word of God in the church today. Schismatic sectarianism (the division of Christians into multiple religious denominations) is the fulfillment of scriptural prophecy; "The kings of the earth set themselves, and the rulers take counsel together, against the Lord, and against his anointed, *saying*, Let us break their bands asunder, and cast away their cords from us" (Psalm 2:2–3). There are some stadium-sized megachurch-

---

19 John Hagee Ministries, May/June 2018 publication.

20 "51% of Churchgoers Don't Know of the Great Commission." Barna Group. Accessed May 22, 2018. https://www.barna.com/research/half-churchgoers-not-heard-great-commission/.

es which claim to be Christian, yet will not even mention Jesus Christ, sin, or hell. Their focus is on humanism—emphasizing the power of individuals to save themselves through positive thinking—while ignoring the grace of Deity to forgive through repentance, and acceptance of a personal Savior in Jesus Christ as the substitutionary sacrifice. They teach that being good and doing good works is all that's needed to get to heaven. This strategy of Satan teaches people to think that their (few) good works will outweigh their (many) bad thoughts and deeds, and thereby tip the balance of salvation in their favor. It completely contradicts New Testament teaching that "For by grace are ye saved through faith; and that not of yourselves: *it is* the gift of God" (Ephesians 2:8). It also ignores Old Testament wisdom "But we are all as an unclean *thing*, and all our righteousnesses *are* as filthy rags; and we all do fade as a leaf; and our iniquities, like the wind, have taken us away" (Isaiah 64:6). Original sin is inherent in all of us and can only be cleansed by the shed blood of Jesus Christ on the cross. Outside of Christ, we can do *nothing* to save ourselves, no matter how good we may try to be.

Other feel-good religions tend to promote wellness through acceptance of often-hedonistic lifestyles. "If it feels good, do it, and be at peace while doing it," is their philosophy. Some have called it "no-cost Christianity." Christian theologian J. I. Packer says that "when modern Western man turns to religion (if he does—most don't), what he wants is total tickling relaxation, the sense of being at once soothed, supported, and effortlessly invigorated: in short, hot tub religion."[21] It is meant to make people *feel* good rather than actually *being* good. It is a deception meant to eliminate the guilt of sin, without the removing or repenting of actual sin—to explain and justify their sin rather than confess it and turn from it.

Other churches preach an unscriptural doctrine of forgiveness and inclusion for *all*. It is referred to as Christian Universalism. Its main tenet is that all will be accepted into heaven—regardless of whether or not they die repentant—because God is holy, loving, all-merciful, and all-forgiving. Yet Scripture is perfectly clear that most will *not* gain entry into heaven because they will not

---

21 Packer, J. I. *God's Plans for You*. Crossway Books, 2001. 49

accept Jesus Christ as their personal Savior, and then part with their sinful ways. We read: "Then said one unto him, Lord, are there few that be saved? And he said unto them, Strive to enter in at the strait gate: for many, I say unto you, will seek to enter in, and shall not be able" (Luke 13:23–24); "For many are called, but few are chosen" (Matthew 22:14). Adopting the ways of this secular world deters entry into the spiritual realm of the next world.

God's justice demands punishment for sin. We are all sinners; therefore, we are all guilty and deserving of condemnation. Because we cannot satisfy justice in ourselves, we need the sinless Christ—the Lamb without blemish who took upon Himself our sins and died in our place—to satisfy all the demands of the divine law. Yet many so-called churches ignore this fact and preach foreign doctrines at their peril. Paul the Apostle sternly warned: "As we said before, so say I now again, If any *man* preach any other gospel unto you than that ye have received, let him be accursed" (Galatians 1:9). Belief in salvation without Christ *guarantees* condemnation. That is Satan's specific propaganda campaign designed for those who incline toward religion—to lead them onto false pathways away from Christ's salvation.

You can detect other false gospels being preached if they contradict the Word of God. We read in Leviticus 20:13 "If a man also lie with mankind, as he lieth with a woman, both of them have committed an abomination." Yet we see openly homosexual bishops and ministers preaching acceptance of their lifestyle from the pulpit. They perform same-sex marriages in defiance of God's ordination—from the very beginning—of marriage being between a man and a woman only; "And the rib, which the LORD God had taken from man, made he a woman, and brought her unto the man," (Genesis 2:22). We also see contempt for God's authority in defying His command that "Therefore shall a man leave his father and his mother, and shall cleave unto his wife: and they shall be one flesh," (Genesis 2:24). It is true that we are to love the sinner because we are to love our neighbor as ourselves, and we are *all* sinners. But we are also to hate our sins, and not embrace them or excuse them—no matter *what* they are. "*Let* love be without dissimulation. Abhor that which is evil; cleave to that which is good" (Romans 12:9). We also see divorce freely sanctioned from the pulpit of some churches, despite what Jesus commanded, that "What therefore God hath joined together, let not man put asunder" (Mark 10:9). Today, it seems that any little difference in opinion is considered irreconcilable and therefore qualifies as acceptable grounds for divorce, thereby justifying the breaking of our vows.

These spiritual imposters have used the Trojan Horse military tactic of sneaking into the ministry (through the professed desire to spread the unadulterated Word of God), while concealing their true intent which is either to dilute it, or completely undermine it by mainstreaming sin to make it gradually acceptable; "For such *are* false apostles, deceitful workers, transforming themselves into the apostles of Christ" (2 Corinthians 11:13). It is a feint, a ruse. It is what Senator Daniel Patrick Moynihan described as "defining deviancy down." But upon final judgment, "Many will say to me in that day, Lord, Lord, have we not prophesied in thy name? and in thy name have cast out devils? and in thy name done many wonderful works? And then will I profess unto them, I never knew you: depart from me, ye that work iniquity" (Matthew 7:22-23). Those who alter the Word of God to "modernize" it and make it "progressive" will discover their error in the end—when it is too late, and it becomes an eternal judgment against them.

And then, there are the church businesses run by pastors who operate them solely for their own profit while preaching sacrifice to their congregation. The leaders are hypocrites who adopt a Pharisaical "Do as I say, not as I do" lifestyle. When caught inevitably in compromising situations, they feign remorse as they cry and beg for forgiveness. Unfortunately, as is all too often the case, a sympathetic but deceived church body restores them to duty, only to find out later that "As a dog returneth to his vomit, *so* a fool returneth to his folly" (Proverbs 26:11). The danger these faux pastors pose is that their backsliding may cause many of their flock to lose genuine faith in their own religious beliefs and drift toward a total apostasy. Apostates from religion will receive a greater damnation for having seen the light, yet rejecting it.

Some ministers don't even have a church or congregation. They've been ordained as *Reverends* just to achieve tax-exempt status. They then use their prominent titles to rabble-rouse and sow racial division. We usually see them at the front of political marches trying to look important while they attempt to extort money or favors from the objects of their protests.

Other churches have ordained pedophiles as priests, yet covered up their crimes when exposed in order to keep the clergy fully staffed and the doors open for business. Some of those priests were even promoted to higher duties. In August of 2018, a grand jury report in Pittsburgh, Pennsylvania, named over 300 sexual predator priests in six dioceses as having sexually molested or raped over 1,000 children since the 1950's.[22] The church engaged in a systematic cover-up. These findings parallel previous investigations in Philadelphia and Boston of similar allegations.

Some churches also tend to promote worship by rote and ritual, despite Jesus' warning against religious ritualism; "Howbeit in vain do they worship me, teaching *for* doctrines the commandments of men" (Mark 7:7). Sadly, while many of those parishioners have joined because they do possess a saving faith—be it as small as a mustard seed—the church's ritualism of going through the motions does not water that seed through biblical study and exposition for it to grow into anything larger, lest their faith become self-sufficient through personal prayer and preclude the need for the church to "save" them on a weekly basis, (while passing the basket for donations). Those parishioners become stunted in their understanding of God's Word and His plan for them, and rarely develop any further into purposeful service to Christ. Going to church once a week and performing a ritual is about all the religion they experience in their lives. They are never actually taught the entire Bible and its full significance, and therefore are unable to satisfy the Great Commission given us by Jesus: "Go ye therefore, and teach all nations, baptizing them in the name of the Father, and of the Son, and of the Holy Ghost: Teaching them to observe all things whatsoever I have commanded you" (Matthew 28:19–20). To *preach* the Gospel and the Bible, one must *know and understand* the Gospel and the Bible.

---

[22] "301 'Predator Priests' Named In Pa. Grand Jury Sex Abuse Report: 'They Were Raping Little Boys & Girls.'" CBS Pittsburgh. August 14, 2018. Accessed August 15, 2018. https://pittsburgh.cbslocal.com/2018/08/14/pennsylvania-diocese-sex-abuse-grand-jury-report-released/.

Jesus warned us that "... Every kingdom divided against itself is brought to desolation; and every city or house divided against itself shall not stand" (Matthew 12:25). Sowing discord in the body of the church is all part of Satan's general military strategy to *divide and conquer.*

Anti-religion propaganda promulgated through movies, music, television, etc., also serves to deter God's message of salvation. All too often, the plot of a movie has the devout religious person as the crazed serial killer. Blasphemies taking the name of Jesus Christ in vain seem to appear in every movie without a General Admission rating. (See Chapter Fifteen for further discussion of this, in relation to politics.) Alternate families, in which marriage is not between one man and one woman, are promoted openly as the norm, despite thousands of years of global cultural agreement in the definition of marriage. Musical lyrics promote violence or murder against women, police, and hatred of other races. Paradoxically, these negative messages of hate are rigorously defended and protected under the First Amendment's right to free speech (in America), while messages of Christian love and forgiveness are ruled unconstitutional hate speech, and silenced. Satan has effectively turned the world upside down, but "Woe unto them that call evil good, and good evil; that put darkness for light, and light for darkness; that put bitter for sweet, and sweet for bitter!" (Isaiah 5:20). When Jesus returns, He will right the world.

Know Yourself

It is not enough to know your enemy in order to obtain victory. It is also necessary to know yourself. You must be able to identify honestly your own strengths and weaknesses. More importantly, you must be able to determine the ebbs and flows of those strengths and weaknesses as they constantly fluctuate. Victory against temptation may be achievable on one day due to a renewed vitality to resist, yet elusive on another day due to a drained vulnerability to succumb. God may have delivered you recently from some travail and your current spirit of gratitude is strong, therein rendering Satan's attacks at that time much more unlikely to succeed. Yet, as is usually the case, that gratitude tends to wane over time and may gradually be forgotten. It is then, when the drawbridge to the stronghold is lowered, that the enemy can effectively march in, bypassing the castle wall defenses.

Sun Tzu observed that "If you know the enemy and know yourself, you need not fear the result of a hundred battles. If you know yourself but not the enemy, for every victory gained you will also suffer a defeat. If you know neither the enemy nor yourself, you will succumb in every battle" (*ch.*III, *ss.*18). It is therefore imperative to assess with absolute honesty your situational awareness day by day, even moment by moment. It only takes a single instance of weakness to fall into sin, yet the ramifications of that sin could last a lifetime through consequences such as disease, divorce, or even incarceration. "Watch and pray, that ye enter not into temptation: the spirit indeed *is* willing, but the flesh *is* weak" (Matthew 26:41). Paul the Apostle admitted to not understanding why "For that which I do I allow not: for what I would, that do I not; but what I hate, that do I" (Romans 7:15). If even the great teacher Apostle can be caught off guard, how much more so can we as students?

Satan's attacks are tailor-made to the individual. He first seeks out the essential elements of information—our general weaknesses and vulnerabilities—to obtain a beachhead during the action phase of his assault. He then determines an operational combat plan based upon the changing conditions of our defenses. He assesses the feasibility of success and modifies his plan as needed to account for the momentary changes in our strengths and weaknesses, seeking an aimpoint in order to establish an area of concentration for his barrages. Using the military tactic called swarming, he attempts to overwhelm certain specific weakened defenses with a concentrated zone of fire. Once those defenses are penetrated, he seeks to establish a bridgehead for continued aggression. He plans his future operations against humanity by developing an adversary template for each of us, based upon past successful strategies.

A handy acronym you can use as a reminder to check for potential spiritual vulnerability is HALT, which stands for: Hungry; Angry; Lonely; Tired. These can all act as incapacitating agents. If you are in any one of these states—hunger, anger, loneliness, or fatigue—there is a good chance that your defenses are temporarily weakened, so halt, and think twice before acting once.

We see a perfect example of *hunger* affecting reason and weakening resolve, when Esau came in famished from hunting in the fields. He smelled Jacob's stew and sold his birthright for a bowl of it, as we read in Genesis 25:30–33:

> And Esau said to Jacob, Feed me, I pray thee, with that same red *pottage*; for I *am* faint: therefore was his name called Edom. And Jacob said, Sell me this day thy birthright. And Esau said, Behold, I *am* at the point to die: and what profit shall this birthright do to me? And Jacob said, Swear to me this day; and he sware unto him: and he sold his birthright unto Jacob.

Jewish birthright (known as primogeniture) was bestowed

upon the firstborn son. To him was bequeathed the greater part of the inheritance—a double portion of all the father's possessions; the future position as head over the family and controller of the family property; and a special blessing from the father. Yet he traded it all away for a single bowl of stew because he was momentarily hungry!

It is a medical fact that with proper hydration, severe symptoms of starvation don't appear until after thirty-five to forty days without food. Esau probably had not eaten since only that morning and was therefore nowhere near starving to death. Yet, he devoured Satan's lie that he was near the point of death by exaggerating his hunger, and then succumbed to an immediate gratification to eat. In doing so, he also violated (quite literally) another of Sun Tzu's military maxims "Do not swallow bait offered by the enemy" (*ch*.7, *ss*.35). Hunger also creates irritability and can lead to anger, as we see many people in this condition described nowadays as being "hangry."

Anger also distorts judgment and perception. "Two Greek words in the New Testament are translated as 'anger.' One means 'passion, energy' and the other means 'agitated, boiling.'"[23] The first definition is of a healthy anger, also known as "righteous indignation," such as when Jesus became angry with the moneychangers profaning the temple and then chased them out. But the second definition can lead to spiritual debilitation, as anger hardens our heart. It is a dangerous emotion against which we should be carefully on our guard.

There is a warning in Ephesians 4:26–27: "Be ye angry, and sin not: let not the sun go down upon your wrath: Neither give place to the devil." This proves that Satan will seek to exploit your anger. He may tempt you toward an immediate response to throw out a harsh word at someone to inflict emotional pain. Or he may tempt you to a hostile action that willfully hurts another person over time. Either way, collateral damage can result from a sinful, retaliatory aggression which should be avoided, for it is written: "Dearly beloved, avenge not yourselves, but *rather* give place unto wrath: for it is written, Vengeance *is* mine; I will repay, saith

---

23 GotQuestions.org. "What Does the Bible Say about Anger?" GotQuestions.org. February 21, 2018. Accessed November 17, 2017. https://www.gotquestions.org/Bible-anger.html.

the Lord" (Romans 12:19). If indulged, anger lingers and festers and hinders fellowship with God. It yields Satan a *foot*hold on which he attempts to build a *strong*hold to plant further justifications in our minds for that anger, so that it becomes foundational in canceling out any joy or peace in our lives. Therefore, "Be not hasty in thy spirit to be angry: for anger resteth in the bosom of fools" (Ecclesiastes, 7:9). Knowledge of God's forgiveness extended to us should evoke our forgiveness of others. That is the way to neutralize anger.

Loneliness is a frame of mind. It is a feeling, rather than a physical state of being. One can be married and still be lonely. One can feel lonely in a huge crowd. Loneliness is a sense of being disconnected from others, or from God. As such, it is spiritual problem. "And the LORD God said, *It is* not good that the man should be alone; I will make him an help meet for him" (Genesis 2:18). Satan tries to isolate us from others, just as a lion will seek to isolate its prey by seeking the weakest member of the herd and cutting it off from the others. To combat the sense of isolation, Jesus assured us that "I am with you alway, *even* unto the end of the world" (Matthew 28:20). Let that be a comfort to us—that we are never truly alone. And then let us commune regularly with Jesus to maintain that comfort by His constant presence.

Being *tired* can lead to many dangerous situations, both physical and spiritual. Thousands of motor vehicle accidents are directly attributable to sleep deprivation every year because of the decreased level of alertness leading to a delayed reaction time. An increase in workplace accidents, through a decrease in judgmental skills, has been directly correlated to a lack of sleep in the worker. Fatigue also contributes toward an inability to communicate effectively with others. Exhaustion affects your cognitive abilities to think clearly. When you're tired, your spiritual guard is down, and you become vulnerable to mood disorders such as anger and depression. It should be no surprise then that a tired, distracted soul is vulnerable to attack.

Other states of personal vulnerability include *fear* and *anxiety*. Anything that disturbs our peace becomes a useful inroad for the enemy to encroach upon. Excessive fear, worry, and anxiety can all lead to negative emotional and/or behavioral consequences in our professional and personal relationships. Spiritually, anxiety can cripple our thoughts with the darkness of despair. Where there is little spiritual light, there is little earthly hope. To guard against fear, it is helpful to memorize this scriptural verse: "Fear thou not; for I *am* with thee: be not dismayed; for I *am* thy God: I will strengthen thee; yea, I will help thee; yea, I will uphold thee with the right hand of my righteousness" (Isaiah 41:10). We are never alone. We are never without the promise of protection.

Pride is another condition to be wary of. People may feel strong in spirit, yet their overconfidence can be their undoing. When tested, the pride in their own strength is often proven false. We see a perfect example of that in Peter. When Jesus told the apostles that they would all leave and forsake Him upon His arrest, "Peter answered and said unto him, Though all *men* shall be offended because of thee, *yet* will I never be offended" (Matthew 26:33). Yet, a very short time later, Peter fled the Garden of Gethsemane with the other apostles upon Jesus' arrest, and then, when confronted by others about his affiliation with Jesus, Peter panicked and denied three times that he even knew the Lord. Therefore, as a bulwark against pride, it is very helpful to keep this wisdom in mind at all times: "Wherefore let him that thinketh he standeth take heed lest he fall" (1 Corinthians 10:12). Prayer for strength, through the humility of acknowledged perpetual weakness, is the remedy for a prideful spirit.

Another personal vulnerability to seek out and correct for is *impatience*. The spirit of impatience comes from the devil. Indulging it leads to intolerance, frustration, and anger, thereby providing a stronghold for Satan. People who just can't wait for their turn at anything—whether waiting in line on foot, or driving a car—exhibit a selfish, me-first attitude, and tend to act impetuously upon it through harsh words or selfish deeds which are almost always at someone else's expense. This leads to conflict. Two impatient drivers jockeying for an advantage leads to road-rage incidents in which people have actually been killed in retaliatory confrontation.

Impatience in waiting upon Samuel to appear—as commanded by God in order to offer the holy sacrifice—cost Saul his kingship;

> And Samuel said to Saul, Thou hast done foolishly: thou hast not kept the commandment of the LORD thy God, which he commanded thee: for now would the LORD have established thy kingdom upon Israel for ever. But now thy kingdom shall not continue: the LORD hath sought him a man after his own heart, and the LORD hath commanded him *to be* captain over his people, because thou hast not kept *that* which the LORD commanded thee.
> (1 Samuel 13:13–14)

Impatience, therefore, is also doubt in God's plan for us, and in His perfect timing. When those seeds are sown by Satan, their fruits result in our making rash decisions without due consideration and which ultimately have a negative outcome for us. The tactical solution is to be "Rejoicing in hope; patient in tribulation; continuing instant in prayer" (Romans 12:12). Patience and prayer will deliver us through all adversity.

Confusion is an unsettled state of mind in which the enemy has created doubt and uncertainty to gain spiritual advantage. The inevitable trials and tribulations in our lives can sow confusion as to what God's purpose is for us. Something bad happens to us, and we blame ourselves as if we had deserved it. That is a result of Satan whispering in our ears—trying to convict and punish us for sins we've likely already been forgiven through our repentance.

Promoting confusion in the understanding of Scripture has been a massive and incredibly successful disinformation campaign waged by the enemy. It has led many people throughout the ages to execute abominable acts in the name of religion, thinking they were acting righteously instead. How many people in history have been murdered through a confused, perverted interpretation of Scripture? We need only look at examples such as the Spanish Inquisition to see Satan's success in promoting a misguided holy zeal on the part of those who were scripturally confused. The Bible warns us against this; "... yea, the time cometh, that whosoever killeth you will think that he doeth God service" (John 16:2). We are seeing a lesser example of this today in the political and cultural war being waged against religion—

with the killing of any public religious expression, and the character assassination of the righteous.

We see more subtle forms of religious confusion today through "legalism" in the churches. A strict and literal interpretation of the letter of the Law—emphasizing rules and regulations for salvation, while ignoring the spirit of the Law—is the definition of legalism. It is the doctrinal opposite of saving grace. Jesus railed against the Pharisees in His time for their reliance upon it. He provoked them many times by deliberately healing on the Sabbath (despite their insistence to do *no* work on the Sabbath). Stephen J. Cole observes that "At the root of legalism is the sin of pride, because the legalist thinks that he is able to commend himself to God by his own good deeds. Invariably, he is only looking at externals, not at his heart."[24] Jesus knows the condition of our hearts in all of our actions. It is imperative that we, too, discover the motives behind all we think and do. Are we acting to glorify God or to magnify ourselves?

Realizing that confusion is only a *temporary* condition is the first part of defeating it. Studying and meditating upon Scripture will help dispel the fog of fluster. Prayer for clarity must also follow; "For thou wilt light my candle: the LORD my God will enlighten my darkness" (Psalm 18:28). Through prayer, the enemy's smoke screen of disorientation can be dissipated so that we can see clearly once again.

An often-unsuspected chink in our armor is the presence of *superstition* in our lives. It is an irrational fear of the unknown that can create unhealthy practices in our lives. It cripples us without any basis in sound knowledge or reason. Perceived unfounded ominous portents can cause us both to do unwise things, or, conversely, not to do the wise things we should. As a result, we may rely upon magic (consulting astrologers), or in chance (numerology) to explain and divine the supernatural through a sinful need-to-know attitude, rather than relying upon sound scriptural doctrine and faith in prayer. Sun Tzu also warned against it in his time: "Prohibit the taking of omens, and do away with superstitious doubts" (*ch.*11, *ss.*26). An example of succumbing

---

24 Cole, Steven J. "Lesson 57: Why Jesus Hates Legalism (Luke 11:37-54)." Bible.org. Accessed December 10, 2017. https://bible.org/seriespage/lesson-57-why-jesus-hates-legalism-luke-1137-54.

to this trick of Satan is if you skipped a great job interview because it was scheduled on a Friday the thirteenth. Satan tricked you into missing what may have been God's best for you.

We'll end this chapter with a brief discussion about *appetites of the flesh* and other *inordinate desires* which create gaping holes in our spiritual defenses. They become the back doors for sin to enter in freely. For example, having one drink after working a long day may be acceptable to God, such as drinking some "wine *that* maketh glad the heart of man" (Psalm 104:15). But if it leads to many more drinks, resulting in sloppy drunkenness, then Satan has turned something unobjectionable into something detestable. What people do when they are drunk is often quite shameful. And though one may feel remorse the next day, what was foolishly done or said while drunk usually can't be undone or unsaid, once sober.

Another example can be found in the natural impulse to eat food for daily sustenance being distorted into a gluttonous obsession with food consumption, resulting in morbid obesity. Therefore, moderation is always a sound strategy to pursue in order to avoid the pitfalls of excessive indulgence.

Other perilous conditions that result from excessive passions may include perverting a simple appreciation of the beauty and art form of the human body into a depraved obsession with pornography. Personalities who seek thrills, or have low impulse control, or are depressed and try to manage their emotions, are more prone to engage in risky behavior, and are at higher risk for drug and alcohol addictions. Satan will always seek to exploit those weaknesses in our individual characters. Therefore, special fortifications need to be constructed against identified personal shortcomings to shore up those weaknesses and deny the enemy those areas for conquest.

5

Satan's Arsenal

We've now seen the tactics and strategies of the enemy, but what of his weaponry? He always uses the best weapon for the best result. This means that his attacks on people are particular—using whatever weapons work best against each of us individually. As stated previously, the universal siege weapon he employs against all of us, at all times, is temptation. Since the souls of all of us currently alive are walled in by the fortress of the flesh until death, we are all vulnerable to the spiritual attrition of constant temptation. It is through the spiritual fortifications breached by temptation that other weapons are then discharged and whole arrays of sins are subsequently committed. Therefore, we should study his generalized use of that preliminary tactic first, before exploring the subsequent use of his specialized armaments against us.

Temptation is an inducement to commit sin. By itself, it is not yet a sin (even Jesus was tempted by Satan); but succumbing to it is. In yielding to it, we are making a conscious decision to indulge a forbidden desire through a certain course of action. It always starts in the mind as an enticing thought planted by the enemy. The longer the dwell time we invest upon this appealing propaganda, the more steadily we progress into enemy territory until we end up in Satan's minefield where any forward or lateral movement may be hazardous. Instead of entertaining the initial thought, it is better to identify it immediately as a perilous road to destruction by looking beyond the immediate allurements to see, instead, the consequences awaiting us at the end of that route; "Casting down imaginations, and every high thing that exalteth itself against the knowledge of God, and bringing into captivity every thought to the obedience of Christ" (2 Corinthians 10:5). In that way, the battle is fought and won through a tactical interdiction in the mind to prevent engagement of the body's complicity in the sinful action. Therefore, the best strategy is always to avoid identified hostile environments. But if we do suddenly find ourselves in some minefield, then it is best to slowly back out of it the way we came in—the obvious examples being that, if you're on a diet, you shouldn't frequent food courts, or hang around with your friends in bars if you're a recovering alcoholic. Depart those hostile environments before stepping on the buried landmines of gluttony or drunkenness. That same strategy of restraint should be applied to every identified and recorded personal weakness. English minister and biblical expositor Matthew Henry (1662–1714) wrote that "Those that would avoid sin must not parley with temptation."[25] This is sound advice. If you don't want to get burned eternally, don't play with hell's fire.

The greatest defense against temptation, however, can be found in the Bible. It is written that if we pray for strength at the moment of weakness, God will provide that escape for us. Scripture assures us that "There hath no temptation taken you but such as is common to man: but God *is* faithful, who will not suffer you to be tempted above that ye are able; but will with the temptation also make a way to escape, that ye may be able to bear *it*" (1 Corinthians 10:13). A healthy knowledge of the Word will provide specific verses as leverage against specific temptations as well, as we see Jesus quoting them in His battle over the various temptations of the devil in the wilderness, recorded in Matthew 4:1–11.

Guilt is another favored weapon of the devil. True guilt involves realizing your sin, and then feeling remorse over committing it. Satan will torment us endlessly over it, if we yield him that spiritual ground by forgetting that God will forgive us if we repent it. It is written that "the blood of Jesus Christ his Son

---

25 Henry, Matthew. *Matthew Henry's Commentary on the Whole Bible: Wherein Each Chapter Is Summed up in Its Contents, Each Paragraph Reduced to Its Proper Heads, the Sense Given, and Largely Illustrated with Practical Remarks and Observations: Genesis to Revelation.* Peabody, MA: Hendrickson Publishers, 1991. Vol. 4, 814.

cleanseth us from all sin" (1 John 1:7). This is also confirmed in 1 John 1:9, which states that "If we confess our sins, he is faithful and just to forgive us *our* sins, and to cleanse us from all unrighteousness." Though these verses provide those with a stronger faith the military posture to deter that aggression, those with a weaker faith are still left vulnerable. Satan seeks out those who don't fully believe in the promise of Scripture and therefore feel undeserving and unconvinced of their forgiveness. He then wages an attack relying upon *false* guilt. It is a form of double jeopardy in which a person is wrongfully prosecuted *twice* for the *same* offense. If we have acknowledged our guilt *once* through the conviction of the Holy Spirit, and have done a proper battle damage assessment leading to repentance of our sin before God through Jesus Christ our Advocate, then we are fully absolved of it and Satan has no legal authority to charge us with it again. "Get thee hence, Satan" (Matthew 4:10) should be our immediate, justified response.

A similar weapon employed against us is *shame*. "While guilt is seeing what you've done, shame is seeing yourself as a failure because of what you've done. Guilt is looking at the sin, shame is looking at yourself. If you allow yourself to meditate upon guilt, it will turn into shame. Guilt, if not properly dealt with, turns into a stronghold called shame."[26] While godly shame is a useful conviction tool to bring about repentance and change from a sinful lifestyle or attitude, relentless and unforgiving satanic shame lowers self-esteem and confidence, and allows the enemy a propaganda stronghold to undermine us from within. The deceitful message he incessantly delivers is that we are not worthy to approach the throne of God and offer our service to Him—with the intent of keeping us away from communion with God through prayer, and from communion with fellow believers in the church body—and therein erode our usefulness by reducing our spiritual fortifications through isolation. It is part of his divide-and-conquer strategy.

Yet, we can take solace in Hebrews 9:14. "How much more shall the blood of Christ, who through the eternal Spirit of-

---

26 *Spiritual warfare: Defeating guilt and shame*, accessed December 24, 2017, http://www.greatbiblestudy.com/sws_guilt_shame.php

fered himself without spot to God, purge your conscience from dead works to serve the living God?" Biblical verses, such as this one, assure us that the persecuting shame of our sins should be put away when the sin is put away, and we are cleansed of it through repentance. If St. Paul, who before his conversion had many Christians put to death, could say "I thank God, whom I serve from *my* forefathers with pure conscience ..." (2 Timothy 1:3), then who are we to reject God's forgiveness by dwelling in a shame which should have been washed away along with the pardoned sin? That perceived wall of shame before us is, in actuality, only a shadow—a phantom construct without substance, a battlefield deception.

Regret is another inroad Satan uses to undermine our defenses. Some regret can be mended through certain corrective action, such as an apology. But that is more akin to repentance. Oppressive regret over past bad decisions in our lives can rob us, through a spirit of disappointment, of the current joy promised us by God as forgiven, repentant sinners. Firm belief in Romans 8:28, "And we know that all things work together for good to them that love God, to them who are the called according to *his* purpose," will provide us an active defense against the false notion that we can never stop suffering from our past mistakes. While it may be true that in making some bad decisions we forfeited God's best for us at the time, He will make allowances and still offer us alternate (though possibly lesser) options to obtain good results from our failures.

Another of Satan's favorite strategies is to employ an all-purpose weapon containing multiple munitions to cause indiscriminate area effects over a broad range of personal weaknesses. This type of cluster bomb is the generalized grouping of the so-called "seven deadly sins" which, upon detonation, impacts all particularly vulnerable areas of weakness. Pride, envy, gluttony, lust, anger, greed, and sloth provide a target-rich environment for the enemy to assail and thereby impair defenses and hinder development of spiritual maturity.

Pride leads to a haughty spirit and is often called the "sin of sins." It was what led to Lucifer's downfall, paving the way for all other sins. It creates an illusion of self-grandeur by obscuring the truth, and therein promotes rivalry between us and God for glory. It elevates the self above others, even though "... there is no respect of persons with God" (Romans 2:11), and "How much less to him that accepteth not the persons of princes, nor regardeth the rich more than the poor? for they all *are* the work of his hands" (Job 34:19). In God's eyes, we are all the same. If in our own eyes we see ourselves as elevated above others, then we have succumbed to the sin of pride, and we can expect a reckoning, for "Pride *goeth* before destruction, and an haughty spirit before a fall" (Proverbs 16:18). The defense against pride is humility, obtained by praying for a proper perspective of who we are, and of our place in the universe under an all-powerful, all-knowing God. It is written in James 4:6 "Wherefore he saith, God resisteth the proud, but giveth grace unto the humble." Therefore, "A man's pride shall bring him low: but honour shall uphold the humble in spirit" (Proverbs 29:23). Let us never elevate ourselves above others. If Jesus can wash the feet of His disciples, who are we to refuse to do likewise?

Envy is a desire to have what others have. It could involve material possessions, societal or workplace position, favor in the eyes of others, etc. It "is unlikeness to God ... an opposition and contradiction to God; it is a dislike of His proceedings, and a displeasure at what He does, and is pleased with."[27] It was the sin that led to the first recorded murder in the Bible, when Cain murdered Abel over God's favor. It stems from unhappiness in one's situation. Psychologists identify two types of envy: benign and malicious. Benign envy can motivate positive change. Malicious envy is Satan's weapon. "A sound heart *is* the life of the flesh: but envy the rottenness of the bones" (Proverbs 14:30). Contentment and proper thanksgiving to God for what we have (counting our blessings) will dissipate jealousy and envy, and give us a peaceful soul.

Gluttony is an inordinate desire to eat or drink more than is necessary. Gluttony idolizes food and/or drink, and, in effect, makes a god of our belly. This is a subtle form of idolatry which robs God of worship and glory in favor of the food offering on the altar of the dining table. We tend to justify it by claiming

---

[27] Henry, *Commentary*, Vol. 5, 231.

that we *need* to eat, therefore it is legal to do so. Because of that, it is probably (for Christians) the most tolerated sin of the big seven listed above. James Faris notes that in *Summa Theologica* Part 2-2, Question 148:4, Thomas Aquinas and Gregory the Great identified five types of gluttony: eating too soon; eating too expensively; eating too much; eating too daintily (picky eaters); and eating too eagerly.[28] Gluttony often leads to us into a quicksand-trap of guilt. We overeat and then often hate ourselves for doing it, yet repeat the cycle endlessly. As we continue to squirm in that mire, we sink—overcome eventually by heart disease, diabetes, or other health-related ailments which are directly attributable to obesity. It is the enemy's relentless siege upon our soul which lessens the resistance of the defender—not by cutting off essential supplies but by overindulgence of available supplies—in order to repeat the sin of Israel's gluttonous desire for quail, which was their undoing as well. "And while the flesh *was* yet between their teeth, ere it was chewed, the wrath of the LORD was kindled against the people, and the LORD smote the people with a very great plague" (Numbers 11:33). God had supplied Israel with heavenly manna, yet they desired meat in their ingratitude instead. We can expect nothing good from succumbing to gluttony.

The solution is to practice moderation and to exercise self-control by seeing food for what it truly is meant for: sustenance. Diet and exercise will help destroy gluttony in our lives. To fortify us spiritually, it is also helpful to remember that "All things are lawful unto me, but all things are not expedient: all things are lawful for me, but I will not be brought under the power of any" (1 Corinthians 6:12). We are warned of the fate of gluttons "Whose end *is* destruction, whose God *is their* belly, and *whose* glory *is* in their shame, who mind earthly things" (Philippians 3:19). So instead, "... put ye on the Lord Jesus Christ, and make not provision for the flesh, to *fulfil* the lusts *thereof*" (Romans 13:14). Let us not be enticed by the enemy to make a god of anything carnal, but instead hold fast to our Lord and Savior, Jesus Christ.

Lust is a strong desire for something which is forbidden or

---

28 James Faris, "Is the Sin of Gluttony Really that Serious?" accessed January 14, 2018, https://www.crosswalk.com/church/pastors-or-leadership/is-the-sin-of-gluttony-really-that-serious.html

harmful to us. Whereas gluttony is probably the most tolerated sin, lust is likely the most prevalent sin as it comes in many forms, such as the desire for material possessions; money; knowledge; position; power; food and drink—as well as sexual desires. Throughout history it has led to divorce, murder, disease epidemics, and war—as well as the fall of humanity into sin in the Garden of Eden. We are cautioned to avoid it in nearly every book of the Bible in both the Old and New Testaments.

Lust in the Bible usually refers to sexual sin. Sexual desire in itself is not a sin. God created it within us to urge procreation. But He also gave us guidelines to do so within a marital union to strengthen its ties. Sex outside of that relationship becomes the sin of lust. It is what Satan seeks to entice us with. Indulging it is a willful choice on our part. Contrary to what many feel is acceptable, lusting with the eye—even without committing the act—is still sinful. Jesus clearly stated in Matthew 5:27-28 "Ye have heard that it was said by them of old time, Thou shalt not commit adultery: But I say unto you, That whosoever looketh on a woman to lust after her hath committed adultery with her already in his heart." To avoid the lust of the eyes, we should do as Job 31:1: "I made a covenant with mine eyes; why then should I think upon a maid?" We are commanded in Galatians 5:16 "*This* I say then, Walk in the Spirit, and ye shall not fulfil the lust of the flesh." Because lust is an example of asymmetric warfare upon our souls—through the burdening flesh we humans cannot escape—overcoming it requires us to employ secret weapons, and an appeal to a stronger ally. As stated previously in Chapter Three, our secret weapon is prayer. Our all-powerful ally is Christ. Praying for strength in times of weakness will fortify our spiritual barriers against the assault through a joint operation with the Spirit.

Anger sets reason aside in favor of fury. Instead of becoming enraged, "seeing red" should act as an early-warning indicator light of the enemy's approach. Once alerted, we can prepare a guard against issuing hasty vitriolic speech by disciplining our tongue in advance—for anger begets anger. "A soft answer turneth away wrath: but grievous words stir up anger" (Proverbs 15:1). American author Ambrose Bierce (1842-1914) once wrote: "Speak when you are angry and you will make the best speech you will ever regret." As we have already explored in Chapter Four under HALT conditions, not all anger (righteous indignation) is bad. When it becomes a *self*-righteous wrath against others, however, it then becomes sin as it leads to bitterness and an unforgiving spirit. If we are prone to anger easily, we need to formulate a plan of emergency preparedness—measures taken in advance to reduce the duration and effects of anger "... lest *there be* debates, envyings, wraths, strifes, backbitings, whisperings, swellings, tumults" (2 Corinthians 12:20). In Jesus' three-and-a-half *years* of ministry, we only read of a few times in which He became angry. And in each instance, His anger was an expression of righteous indignation directed at either the moneychangers in the temple, or the Pharisees for misguiding the people. If "The Lord *is* slow to anger" (Nahum 1:3), then how much more so should we be, who probably get angry at least three or four times *daily*?

The way to combat anger is first to get to the root of the problem. Seek to understand where the anger comes from. Is it justified, or simply a matter of insulted personal pride? Does the situation require consideration from other viewpoints to justify the actions/words that created the anger? Then we need to reconcile that anger with what is written in the Bible, foremost, that anger and vengeance belong to God, and that He sees all unrighteousness perpetrated against us. "Dearly beloved, avenge not yourselves, but rather give place unto wrath: for it is written, Vengeance is mine; I will repay, saith the Lord" (Romans 12:19). Knowing that every injustice will be handled in due time, we then must adhere to Jesus' teaching "For if ye forgive men their trespasses, your heavenly Father will also forgive you" (Matthew 6:14). American general George Catlett Marshall (1880–1959) once said that "Military power wins battles, but spiritual power wins wars." So, just as Jesus said "Peace, be still" (Mark 4:39) to quiet the storm, we can halt the progress of our anger by praying for Jesus to calm those raging winds and seas within us as well, and He will.

Like gluttony and lust, *greed* is also a sin of desire. It is usually regarded as the passionate longing to accumulate material possessions and/or wealth beyond what is necessary. Though we may have enough, the enemy instills a spirit of dissatisfaction through an insatiable desire for more and more, thereby undermining our happiness. In Matthew 6:25-33, Jesus instructed us not to worry about our daily needs. Like the other seven deadly sins, greed, too, gives rise to other sins "For the love of money is the root of all evil" (1 Timothy 6:10). Note that it is not money itself which is the root of all evil, but the inordinate *love* of it.

One great sin which follows as a result of greed is distrust in God. The Lord provided for the Israelites in the desert with heavenly manna for forty years. But He also gave them instructions for collecting it. They were to gather only enough to suffice for each day (excepting a double portion gathered for the upcoming Sabbath). Anything else collected over and beyond what was needed, rotted and stank, and became infested with maggots overnight. God was teaching a lesson to His people against greed, and for us to trust Him for our daily provisions. Therefore, gathering a double portion when unnecessary was an expression of distrust in God's promise to maintain us. The material things of this world can never satisfy the desires of the soul, so greed also fuels a disavowal of God and the spiritual nature of humanity. To emphasize this point, Jesus gave us the parable of the rich fool who hoarded his bountiful harvest instead of sharing it with others. He made plans to build bigger barns to store it in, yet died that very night. "So *is* he that layeth up treasure for himself, and is not rich toward God" (Luke 12:21). As the saying goes, you'll never see a hearse towing a U-Haul. You can't take it with you. God expects us to be good stewards of His blessings by sharing them, and not to be miserly hoarders of them.

Greed is also a form of money-worshipping idolatry. It got the Israelites into trouble with the golden calf incident in Exodus 32. It creates cracks in our spiritual fortifications which compromise the integrity of our spiritual resolve. The very first of the Ten Commandments states that "Thou shalt have no other gods before me" (Exodus 20:3). It has been proven that having more money—rising beyond the basic needs for food, shelter, and clothing—does not bring happiness and contentment. In fact, it has been shown that suicide risks are actually higher in wealthier neighborhoods. Jesus said that "No man can serve two masters:

for either he will hate the one, and love the other; or else he will hold to the one, and despise the other. Ye cannot serve God and mammon" (Matthew 6:24). *Mammon* in Syriac means "money" or "riches." And therein lies the danger—for the one who loves to pursue, obtain, and gather money will hate God's demand to part with it in charity to others.

The defense against succumbing to greed can be found in this firm belief: "But my God shall supply all your need according to his riches in glory by Christ Jesus" (Philippians 4:19). Developing a spirit of gratitude for what we have, as well as a spirit of generosity to share our bounty with others, will dispel greed. This can be further achieved by the realization that once you have accepted Jesus Christ as your Lord and Savior by repenting of your sins, you are washed clean of them and have become an heir to a heavenly inheritance far beyond any earthly wealth imaginable. You have already won life's lottery on earth. There is no greater wealth obtainable, and it is banked eternally.

Sloth is the avoidance of physical and/or spiritual work. It is a laziness of body and soul resulting from a desire for ease. Physically, it is in direct opposition to the Old Testament command for us to "Be fruitful" (Genesis 1:28). Spiritually, it is in direct opposition to the New Testament command for us to "work out [our] own salvation" (Philippians 2:12), for "The soul of the sluggard desireth, and hath nothing: but the soul of the diligent shall be made fat" (Proverbs 13:4). Therefore, it is a useful weapon Satan employs to achieve his objective of keeping people from attaining the best God has to offer us while on earth in this life, but especially in keeping us from the splendor of the kingdom of heaven in the next life. American pastor and author Brian Hedges identifies four basic characteristics of sloth: (1) carelessness, (2) unwillingness to act, (3) half-hearted effort, and (4) becoming easily discouraged by difficulties.[29]

Carelessness can be combated by cultivating a spirit of excellence instead. Striving to do our best at everything we do, utilizing the talents and abilities given us by God, instills a sense of accomplishment and a healthy self-esteem by efficiently con-

---

29 Brian G. Hedges, *Hit List: Taking Aim at the Seven Deadly Sins* (Minneapolis: Cruciform, 2014), 63.

cluding the task at hand. "And whatsoever ye do, do *it* heartily, as to the Lord, and not unto men" (Colossians 3:23). The immediate rewards are self-evident. The long-term rewards may remain yet to be seen, but we can take hope from Daniel's experience: "Then this Daniel was preferred above the presidents and princes, because an excellent spirit *was* in him; and the king thought to set him over the whole realm" (Daniel 6:3). Though we may not expect to be as elevated as Daniel was in his time, promotions and advancements in life are definitely some of the fruits of careful application.

Every day, we face circumstances in which we can help others. Whether it is simply to speak a kind word to someone who is hurting, or to leave a generous tip to someone who may be struggling financially, or to offer a ride to someone who is stranded—the opportunities abound. An *unwillingness to act* in that regard defies Jesus, who said: "A new commandment I give unto you, That ye love one another; as I have loved you, that ye also love one another" (John 13:34). If we love each other, we will help each other. "Therefore to him that knoweth to do good, and doeth *it* not, to him it is sin" (James 4:17). A healthy and active God-aware conscience will notify us of opportunities to help others, and convict us of deliberately missed opportunities to do so.

It is also a sin to put off habitually and intentionally what needs to be done. *Procrastination* is the art of making excuses to justify laziness. "The sluggard will not plow by reason of the cold; therefore shall he beg in harvest, and have nothing" (Proverbs 20:4). Students who procrastinate on doing homework, studying, or writing papers tend to fail their classes. People who procrastinate in matters of business risk being fired (if working for someone else), or of becoming bankrupt (if they own the business). Spiritual procrastinators who say, "I'll get religion later," or plan on death-bed conversions, most likely end up in hell—eternally separated from God. A countermeasure to employ against procrastination is to look beyond it to see the potential for catastrophe it will yield. Fixate, then, on the worst possible outcomes of your procrastination so as to motivate yourself into action now.

Half-heartedness is a lack of zeal. Spiritually, it is condemning. Jesus chastised the church in Laodicea: "So then because thou art lukewarm, and neither cold nor hot, I will spue thee out of my mouth" (Revelation 3:16). We have seen the consequences of half-heartedness throughout the Old Testament, with Israel losing their fervor for God and then backsliding into sin. We all risk the same dangers today. Therefore, developing a wholehearted love for God and Christ will fortify the work of the Spirit within us and convict us through conscience when we are feeling less zealous than we should be.

Discouragement is surrendering to difficulty. Difficulties in life abound as a matter of fact. Jesus confirmed that "In the world ye shall have tribulation" (John 16:33). Therefore yielding to discouragement is a cowardly form of avoiding reality, rather than confronting it. Evangelical Christian pastor Charles R. Swindoll noted that "Life is 10 percent what happens to you and 90 percent how you react to it." The way to combat discouragement is to view the difficulty as a challenge instead, to be taken head-on, and employ a spirit of competition to overcome the challenge and to excel.

In all the manifestations of sloth, the results are the same. Through laziness, we deny ourselves that which is meant for our good. Sometimes this also entails bringing unnecessary evil consequences upon ourselves through that inaction. This is Satan's desired result, that we embrace his deception of pleasurable ease, and thereby destroy ourselves by not attending to important matters. Yet, it is God's intention "That ye be not slothful, but followers of them who through faith and patience inherit the promises" (Hebrews 6:12). Studying the Word of God will fortify our faith so that "For whatsoever is born of God overcometh the world: and this is the victory that overcometh the world, *even* our faith" (1 John 5:4). Let it not become necessary to ask, "How long wilt thou sleep, O sluggard? when wilt thou arise out of thy sleep?" (Proverbs 6:9). Instead, get up, shake off the grogginess, and get to work!

Another powerful weapon in Satan's arsenal is *concession*, or what American pastor Dr. Charles Stanley calls "The landmine of compromise."[30] *Compromise* can be defined as meeting someone half-way. This means that we acknowledge partial defeat by ac-

---

30   In Touch Ministries daily devotional, October 6, 2017

cepting standards that are lower than desirable. Sometimes this can be good for both parties, such as in ceasing mutual military aggression and establishing peace treaties. Yet, since Satan never desires peace and is always at war with us, compromising with him simply yields spiritual ground to him with no benefit to us at all. God wishes us to be holy in all things. Satan wishes us to be unholy in all things. The two are diametrically opposed. Compromise gives Satan a diplomatic seat at a negotiating table which should not exist. There can be *no* negotiations whatsoever, because sinning against God is non-negotiable to the devout. We are commanded in Ephesians 5:11 "And have no fellowship with the unfruitful works of darkness, but rather reprove *them*." Compromise is an expression of disobedience which then becomes a slippery slope. For once we start down that path in making concessions for sin, tolerating it in our lives becomes easier and easier until it becomes a way of life—all because we allowed Satan to establish a foothold by yielding that spiritual ground to him. Matthew Henry wrote that "the garrison that sounds a parley is not far from being surrendered."[31] Jesus warned the church at Pergamum, "Repent; or else I will come unto thee quickly, and will fight against them with the sword of my mouth" (Revelation 2:16). That church had been tolerating evil within its ranks and was strongly reproved for it.

Avoiding compromise therefore requires establishing a clear line of sight on its cause, to answer the question of why we are tempted. Are we succumbing to outside pressure, or yielding to inward desire? Conceding to the pressure of outside arguments is to act in error on the false intel of the enemy; therefore, it should be rejected outright. To avoid succumbing to inward desire, we need to study the wisdom of Solomon, so that "Discretion shall preserve thee, understanding shall keep thee" (Proverbs 2:11), and then respond to the early warning system of the Holy Spirit. We must always remember to "Submit yourselves therefore to God. Resist the devil, and he will flee from you" (James 4:7). By practicing that military tactic of disengagement, we can be delivered from the temptation to compromise with the enemy.

---

31 Henry, *Commentary*, Vol. 1, 18.

Complacency is a sense of "self-satisfaction especially when accompanied by unawareness of actual dangers or deficiencies"[32] It is another powerful weapon of the enemy because of its subtlety. It stealthily encroaches upon us during times of peace in our lives, when we suspect no attack. It drains our zeal, which keeps us from trying harder to grow spiritually stronger. It is neglecting to maintain and build upon the existing spiritual fortifications so that they slowly begin to crumble, fall into ruin, and leave us vulnerable. "Because thou sayest, I am rich, and increased with goods, and have need of nothing; and knowest not that thou art wretched, and miserable, and poor, and blind, and naked" (Revelation 3:17). Dr. James Emory White identifies five marks of complacency: 1) Being far too easily satisfied (over minor achievements); 2) Being quick to make excuses (offering justifications for accepting the stagnant status quo); 3) Acting as if you never have enough time (through a façade of meaningful activity); 4) Feeling as if you are no longer teachable (displaying a pride of existing knowledge); 5) Being content with early success (allowing the fire of perseverance to die).[33] When we feel that we can rest in our *own* strength, wealth, or accomplishments is when we forget that all we have comes from God. "But thou shalt remember the LORD thy God: for *it is* he that giveth thee power to get wealth" (Deuteronomy 8:18). That is Satan's strategy—to keep us from acknowledging the grace of God in our lives, therein cutting off the spiritual supply line to sap our strength. The Bible warns us against this infiltrating evil: "The wicked, through the pride of his countenance, will not seek *after God*: God *is* not in all his thoughts" (Psalm 10:4). In that condition, we have become distracted from our service to God in His plan for us, and have strayed from completing our spiritual mission.

Jesus gave the church two prescriptions to combat complacency. The first is to realize your perilous situation: "... anoint thine eyes with eyesalve, that thou mayest see" and "be zealous therefore, and repent" (Revelation 3:18–19). The second was: "And let

---

32 https://www.merriam-webster.com/dictionary/complacency

33 James Emory White, "Five Marks of Complacency," accessed January 26, 2018, https://www.christianity.com/blogs/dr-james-emery-white/five-marks-of-complacency.html

us consider one another to provoke unto love and to good works: Not forsaking the assembling of ourselves together, as the manner of some is; but exhorting *one another*: and so much the more, as ye see the day approaching" (Hebrews 10:24–25). Attending church services regularly will provide us the opportunity for mutual encouragement, through prayer and Bible study, to keep us sound and recharge any former zeal we may have lost.

One final weapon I'd like to discuss (out of the ever-increasing arsenal of Satan's weaponry) is the use of *counterfeiting*. Throughout history, currency is probably the least considered, though most valuable wartime weapon. Without financial support, wartime efforts cannot be sustained in order to achieve total victory. Therefore, printing counterfeit money has become an often-employed trick to devalue the enemy's currency and thereby undermine their war effort.

Because this is a spiritual battle and economics are not necessarily paramount to victory, Satan instead employs counterfeit friends and ministers to act as double agents—pretending allegiance to one side while secretly advancing the other, whether wittingly or unwittingly. We see this manifested in faulty advice from our intimates, and false doctrines promulgated in the church.

The key to defeating counterfeits is in immediate detection. When friends or family offer advice that is contrary to God's written word, it is a counterfeit currency offered them by the devil. This currency is most often delivered through non-believers, though it may also come from unwary Christians themselves. In moments of spiritual weakness, Satan can temporarily confuse others to act as unwitting agents in his deceit. In that case, friends become foes. We've seen this with the exchange between Peter and Jesus:

> From that time forth began Jesus to shew unto his disciples, how that he must go unto Jerusalem, and suffer many things of the elders and chief priests and scribes, and be killed, and be raised again the third day. Then Peter took him, and began to rebuke him, saying, Be it far from thee, Lord: this shall not be unto thee. But he

turned, and said unto Peter, Get thee behind me, Satan: thou art an offence unto me: for thou savourest not the things that be of God, but those that be of men. (Matthew 16:21–23)

Under the temporary influence of Satan, Peter sought to dissuade the Lord from undergoing His specific mission toward the sacrificial redemption of humanity. If even Peter can fall prey to Satan's influence in criticizing the perfection of the Lord's actions—despite their special religious relationship—then how much more must we be on our guard against this type of personal counterfeit advice as well? In matters of the Spirit, it is imperative to identify the fluctuating status of friend or foe.

And then there are the truly counterfeit so-called "Christians" who exist as devil's advocates—the most prominent example being one of the original apostles. Despite having lived with Jesus and witnessing firsthand the many miracles He performed proving Himself to be the Son of God and Messiah, Judas Iscariot still willingly betrayed his Lord and Savior through the deceitful influence of the enemy. We read in Luke 22:3-43 "Then entered Satan into Judas surnamed Iscariot, being of the number of the twelve. And he went his way, and communed with the chief priests and captains, how he might betray him unto them." Also, in John 13:2 "And supper being ended, the devil having now put into the heart of Judas Iscariot, Simon's *son*, to betray him." (We've covered much of this before under the heading of spiritual imposters, in Chapter Three.)

Counterfeit churches are identifiable through the messages they regularly preach. Do they often speak of sin and hell to constantly warn us off it, or do they instead offer humanistic peace? Does the pastor convict you of your sins, or console you with them? "For when they shall say, Peace and safety; then sudden destruction cometh upon them, as travail upon a woman with child; and they shall not escape" (1 Thessalonians 5:3). Jesus warned: "Think not that I am come to send peace on earth: I came not to send peace, but a sword" (Matthew 10:34). Satan is subtle, and will try to infiltrate the church to pollute the doctrine. We've seen this in Acts 5 in the examples of Ananias and

Sapphira acting as Satan's advance guard in the fledgling church after Pentecost. Therefore, diligently study the Word, and compare what you're hearing with what you've read. If they are irreconcilable, then identify the counterfeit message being preached as a campaign of disinformation. Reject it, and you will be kept safe.

6

Defend Yourself

Though Satan's arsenal is indeed mighty, we must not become dismayed into thinking we are outgunned and overmatched so as to lose any hope of victory. "But the Lord is faithful, who shall stablish you, and keep you from evil" (2 Thessalonians 3:3). There are ways to protect ourselves with a Kevlar-like shield against his various projectiles, thereby neutralizing their effect and rendering us impervious to his assaults. Paul the Apostle adjures us:

> Finally, my brethren, be strong in the Lord, and in the power of his might. Put on the whole armour of God, that ye may be able to stand against the wiles of the devil. For we wrestle not against flesh and blood, but against principalities, against powers, against the rulers of the darkness of this world, against spiritual wickedness in high *places*. Wherefore take unto you the whole armour of God, that ye may be able to withstand in the evil day, and having done all, to stand.
> (Ephesians 6:10–13)

We must properly equip ourselves for battle first, before we can ever hope to make a successful stand in combat. To demonstrate how, Paul enumerates, in order, the procedure in which the Roman soldier dressed for battle. The belt went on first. It had loops for carrying swords, ration sacks, and other equipment; and rings for attaching the breastplate to. "Stand therefore, having your loins girt about with truth, and having on the breastplate of righteousness" (Ephesians 6:14). With the Bible acting as the belt of truth surrounding us at the center of our spiritual being, the gospel itself acts as the buckle of God's objective truth so that religious sincerity and piety will secure and uphold us. The gospel of Christ is true and is to be trusted in all things, at all times.

Belief in Christ's atoning sacrifice on the cross dispels the fog of war between sinful humanity and holy God. With a clear line of sight towards necessary repentance established, and forgiveness attained through the shed blood of Christ, we disable the jamming interference of the enemy's accusations and initiate direct communication with the Lord. An alliance—a new covenant—is forged between us and the forces of righteousness based upon scriptural truth, so that we are protected from the enemy's campaign of confusion and deceit. American theologian Albert Barnes (1798–1870) observed in his commentaries that "A man who has no consistent views of truth, is just the man for the adversary successfully to assail."[34] The truth of the Bible is our cache of spiritual subsistence, and the good conscience against enemy accusations it provides is a supply line of strength that will never fail.

The breastplate of righteousness (integrity, holiness, purity of life, sincerity of piety—as Barnes suggests) will protect and fortify our hearts against the hostile actions of the enemy. Any chink in that armor, via defect of character, is a vulnerability which will certainly become the focal point of attack by Satan. Therefore, "Keep thy heart with all diligence; for out of it *are* the issues of life" (Proverbs 4:23). Abraham had his faith in God accounted to him as righteousness (Genesis 15:6); therefore, our faith in Christ is also imputed to us as righteousness.

Because an unplowed field bears many weeds, we must be industrious in bulldozing it first, before planting that which is godly. We must allow moral rectitude to supersede and replace all unrighteousness in our lives and uproot any worldly weeds of sin. In that way, we can resist every attack through cultivating a militant righteousness.

Paul continues; "And your feet shod with the preparation

---

34 Barnes' Notes on the Bible, accessed January 31, 2018, http://biblehub.com/commentaries/barnes/ephesians/6.htm

of the gospel of peace" (Ephesians 6:15). Roman sandals were embedded with hobnails (cleats) to give the soldier a more secure foothold. We can find sure spiritual footing in the gospel of Christ, so that we will stand firmly with confidence and resolution against Satan's assault, and successfully climb God's holy mountain from the flesh into the Spirit to obtain the military high ground in every battle, for Sun Tzu noted that "All armies prefer high ground to low" (*ch.*IX, *ss.*11). Without the necessary spiritual traction provided us through those cleats, we can be easily pushed into backsliding. A calm heart, resting in the peace and assurance of forgiveness and redemption the gospel offers us, is the key in finding the strength to face with courage any onslaught in combat, and thereby repel any antagonism. "What shall we then say to these things? If God *be* for us, who *can be* against us?" (Romans 8:31). A firm grounding in the good news (gospel) that we are at peace with God, and allied with Him through Jesus Christ, will help us carry the day.

In addition to the other items; "Above all, taking the shield of faith, wherewith ye shall be able to quench all the fiery darts of the wicked" (Ephesians 6:16). In ancient warfare, generally two types of shields were used. One (*clypeus*) was smaller and was worn on the arm to deflect blows in hand-to-hand combat. The other (*scutum*) was larger, and provided full-body coverage for the individual, and, when overlapped with other shields, provided an effective defensive barrier for all the combined troops against incoming missiles such as arrows, spears, and stones. It is this shield which the apostle is making reference to, as oftentimes the enemy would also launch these "darts" with flaming tips to increase their deadly impact. Crouching behind this full-body shield during a withering hail of enemy arrows was an effective defensive measure to keep from impalement, as well as from burning. The fiery darts, which English theologian John Gill (1697–1771) noted, "serve to inflame the mind, and excite to sin, as lust, anger, revenge, and the like,"[35] stick in the impregnable shield, and are then extinguished in the treated leather and wood, thereby keeping the ensconced soldier behind it safe. Faith in our forgiveness and redemption will keep

---

35 Gill's Exposition of the Entire Bible, accessed February 3, 2018, http://biblehub.com/commentaries/gill/ephesians/6.htm

the accusations, recriminations, doubts, and temptations of the enemy from harming us or from passing into sin. The gospel light of truth will dispel all the dark deceit of the enemy if we but hold this shield of faith both high and firm at all times.

Finally, "And take the helmet of salvation, and the sword of the Spirit, which is the word of God" (Ephesians 6:17). The helmet of salvation (or, as in the parallel passage in 1 Thessalonians 5:8, "and for an helmet, the hope of salvation") is the firm knowledge and belief that we are forgiven our sins through faith in Jesus Christ, and therefore will never face separation from God through eternal damnation in hell. Once that saving faith is established—by us *taking* that which God's grace freely offers—we will not fear "them which kill the body, but are not able to kill the soul" (Matthew 10:28). We will not succumb to frets, fears, anxieties, or stresses, but instead will be imbued with a hope—"Which *hope* we have as an anchor of the soul, both sure and stedfast" (Hebrews 6:19)—that conquers despair and temptation; for what soldier can fight as resolutely without the hope of victory? Scottish biblical expositor Alexander MacLaren (1826–1910) wrote: "The consciousness of salvation will tend to damp down the magazine of combustibles that we all carry within us, and the sparks that fall will be as innocuous as those that light on wet gunpowder. If our thoughts are occupied with the blessings which we possess they will be guarded against the assaults of evil. The full cup has no room for poison."[36] The helmet of hope of salvation safeguards us against intellectual surrender and doubt by instilling in us the sure prospect of absolute and total victory. We can then supplement that helmet with the muzzle of purity to guard our tongues against issuing rash speech as well. "Set a watch, O LORD, before my mouth; keep the door of my lips" (Psalm 141:3) so that only sweet waters proceed from our Christian fountain and quench any doubts in our fellow warriors under direct assault as well.

We need to put on the *full* armor of God because the main part of spiritual warfare consists in defense, resistance, and holding our ground—holding "that fast which thou hast, that no man

---

[36] MacLaren Expositions of Holy Scripture, accessed February 4, 2018, http://biblehub.com/commentaries/maclaren/ephesians/6.htm

take thy crown" (Revelation 3:11). Note that there is nothing to cover the back—for the concept of cowardly Christian retreat in warfare is never to be considered an option. "But you will not leave in haste or go in flight; for the LORD will go before you, the God of Israel will be your rear guard" (Isaiah 52:12, NIV).[37] Though there are times when wisdom may dictate a temporary strategic withdrawal, it should be done by slowly backing out of the situation while keeping our eyes focused on the enemy's movements. Cutting and running away in fear only exposes us to disaster. Navigating a calculated disengagement route does not denote a rout.

We now pick up our only offensive weapon in the panoply, the sword of the Spirit. The sword is the Word of God supplied to us by the Holy Spirit. It is a two-edged sword that both cuts and heals by bringing about conviction and repentance in ourselves, as well as in others. "For the word of God *is* quick, and powerful, and sharper than any twoedged sword, piercing even to the dividing asunder of soul and spirit, and of the joints and marrow, and *is* a discerner of the thoughts and intents of the heart" (Hebrews 4:12). It is the only weapon Jesus brandished against Satan's temptations in the desert. We read of the successful results in Matthew 4:10–11 "Then saith Jesus unto him, Get thee hence, Satan: for it is written, Thou shalt worship the Lord thy God, and him only shalt thou serve. Then the devil leaveth him, and, behold, angels came and ministered unto him." Jesus parried Satan's temptations with Scripture and forced him into retreat.

We also see Jesus effectively wielding the sword of Scripture against the Pharisees many times to silence them in their error-ridden, unscriptural attacks upon Him. The sword of the Spirit is the arsenal of scriptural quotations needed to put the enemy to flight. It is a weapon that embodies truth to confront, unmask, and counter the enemy's lies and deceitful errors. With it, we are to assail the enemy boldly to silence the accusing tempter by parrying and deflecting the attack backwards onto him. In 1883, Prussian Field Marshall Colmar Baron von

---

37 New International Version (NIV) Holy Bible, New International Version®, NIV® Copyright © 1973, 1978, 1984, 2011 by Biblica, Inc. ® Used by permission. All rights reserved worldwide.

der Goltz noted that "He who stays on the defensive does not make war, he endures it." Therefore the sword is both an offensive and defensive weapon. "Submit yourselves therefore to God. Resist the devil, and he will flee from you" (James 4:7). For a vivid fictional description of its successful use in battle, read John Bunyan's *Pilgrim's Progress* where, during the fourth stage of Christian's journey, he encounters Apollyon the destroyer, and defeats him in a fight that lasted for more than half a day. We see that to wield the sword of the Spirit effectively, we must first become thoroughly knowledgeable and trained in God's Holy Scripture.

Other defensive armor includes adopting a personal *submission* to the will of God in allowing Him to fight our battles through us in His strength. We must never forget that we possess no courage or fortitude of our own to withstand the enemy's constant onslaught; "Wherefore let him that thinketh he standeth take heed lest he fall" (1 Corinthians 10:12). Therefore, we need to allow God, Christ, and the word of the Holy Spirit to stand for us, and with us in battle. Paul wrote in Romans 8:31 "If God *be* for us, who *can be* against us?" We need also to remember "For the weapons of our warfare *are* not carnal, but mighty through God to the pulling down of strong holds" (2 Corinthians 10:4). Dwelling upon the Word of God—and all the promises and assurances given us within it—will protect us; for the battle is indeed fought in the mind.

Maintaining a posture of *vigilance* will keep our spiritual watchtower manned at all times so that we are never caught at unawares by enemy incursions, however stealthy.

Abstinence will keep us sober from over-indulgence in the staples of life, which lead to stupor and dullness, as well as from the carnal excesses and "... fleshly lusts, which war against the soul" (1 Peter 2:11) and lead to distraction and eventual defeat. Fasting is the denial of the flesh which revives our soul through gaining spiritual clarity.

Finally, "Praying always with all prayer and supplication in the Spirit" (Ephesians 6:18) will keep us focused, spiritually recharged, fully reliant upon and submissive to the higher powers that will ensure victory. *Prayer* covers us with a protective mantle as we petition for the ammunition and weaponry needed to overcome the assault. It fastens all other parts of our armor, and holds us together. An old poem sums it all up accurately:

> *Restraining prayer, we cease to fight;*
> *Prayer makes the Christian armor bright,*
> *And Satan trembles when he sees*
> *The meanest saint upon his knees.*
> *(Author unknown)*

Therefore, pray unceasingly and be victorious.

7

Draw Strength

The best motivation and inspiration for the warrior to win a battle can be provided by reviewing history. The successful experiences of the prophets, Jesus, and the saints, in fighting against the enemy, will strengthen our own resolve. American General Colin Powell stated that "Perpetual optimism is a force multiplier." Arrayed in defense with the full armor of God upon us inspires that necessary optimism to stand firmly in battle, and wielding the sword of Scripture multiplies our offensive force to overcome any assault, as history has proven repeatedly.

Stock market disclaimers warn that past performance is no guarantee of future results, but in spiritual warfare, the exact opposite is true. The armor and weapons used to win battles against Satan throughout history are tested, tried and true, and will always succeed if properly fitted and wielded.

American General Douglas MacArthur (1880–1964) once noted that "It is fatal to enter a war without the will to win it." By studying the past successful strategies of others engaged in spiritual warfare, we can take hope in our own successes as well and develop that necessary will to win so that "No weapon that is formed against thee shall prosper; and every tongue *that* shall rise against thee in judgment thou shalt condemn. This *is* the heritage of the servants of the LORD, and their righteousness *is* of me, saith the LORD" (Isaiah 54:17). Our heritage is spiritual victory through supernatural weapons of intervention.

Some historical references from the Old Testament, of God's prophets praying for deliverance from the enemy's forces, include Isaiah praying for the protection of Israel under King Hezekiah against the invading armies of the Assyrian king, Sennacherib.

"And Isaiah said unto them, Thus shall ye say unto your master, Thus saith the LORD, Be not afraid of the words that thou hast heard, wherewith the servants of the king of Assyria have blasphemed me. Behold, I will send a blast upon him, and he shall hear a rumour, and return to his own land; and I will cause him to fall by the sword in his own land" (Isaiah 37:6–7). By holding fast to God's promises of protection and deliverance, hope was kindled. We read further "And Hezekiah prayed unto the LORD" (Isaiah 37:15). The result was a miraculous divine intercession on behalf of petitioning Israel.

> Then the angel of the LORD went forth, and smote in the camp of the Assyrians a hundred and fourscore and five thousand: and when they arose early in the morning, behold, they *were* all dead corpses. So Sennacherib king of Assyria departed, and went and returned, and dwelt at Nineveh. And it came to pass, as he was worshipping in the house of Nisroch his god, that Adrammelech and Sharezer his sons smote him with the sword.
> (Isaiah 37:36–38)

We learn from this that the prayers of the faithful in times of trial and combat will never go unheeded.

Ezra also relates success in appealing to God; "So we fasted and besought our God for this: and he was intreated of us" (Ezra 8:23). Rather than appeal to Artaxerxes the Persian king for soldiers and horses to protect them as they rebuilt the temple at Jerusalem, Ezra wisely appealed to God instead for protection through prayer and fasting, so that their protection was guaranteed.

Another example (of many) wherein Israel fastened on the full armor of God and wielded the sword of the Spirit through prayer to God occurred when Moab invaded Judah. King Jehoshaphat proclaimed a fast throughout the land and entreated the Lord on behalf of the people. Upon Jahaziel the prophet "... came the Spirit of the LORD in the midst of the congregation; And he said, Hearken ye, all Judah, and ye inhabitants of Jerusalem, and thou king Jehoshaphat, Thus saith the LORD unto you, Be not afraid nor dismayed by reason of this great multitude; for the battle *is* not yours, but God's" (2 Chronicles 20:14-15). We read of the outcome in 2 Chronicles 20:22 "And when they began to sing and to praise, the Lord set ambushments against the children of Ammon, Moab, and mount Seir, which were come against Judah; and they were smitten." We must appeal to the Higher Power in spiritual warfare, to rise above the infirmities of our flesh, in order to gain victory.

Jesus provides many examples of success in personal combat with the enemy, starting in the desert wilderness when Satan presented three great temptations to Him. After fasting for forty days and nights at the commencement of His ministry on earth, He was hungry. Satan tempted Him with an act of self-assertion by distrust in God's provision: "If thou be the Son of God, command that these stones be made bread" (Matthew 4:3). Jesus fended off the blow with the scriptural sword of the Spirit: "But he answered and said, It is written, Man shall not live by bread alone, but by every word that proceedeth out of the mouth of God" (Matthew 4:4). Jesus knew that God has promised us our daily bread, and trusted in that promise. We read that the angels ministered unto Him afterwards.

Satan again tempted Jesus by bringing Him to the top of the temple in the holy city. In his attempt to appeal to human vanity to get Jesus to reveal His divinity through an audacious display, Satan usurped the weapon of Scripture and attempted to wield it against Jesus, "And saith unto him, If thou be the Son of God, cast thyself down: for it is written, He shall give his angels charge concerning thee: and in *their* hands they shall bear thee up, lest at any time thou dash thy foot against a stone" (Matthew 4:6). Again, the blow was successfully parried; "Jesus said unto him, It is written again, Thou shalt not tempt the Lord thy God" (Matthew 4:7). Jesus built His ministry chiefly through teaching and enlightenment of Scripture, with some lessons buttressed by miracles. He came in humility, not in splendor. Revealing Himself outright as the incarnated Son of God at the beginning of His ministry would have precluded the notion of saving faith through grace. Note in the four Gospels, how He always silenced the demons who revealed Him to be the Son of God.

Once more the devil pushed his attack with an all-out assault, offering Jesus dominion over the world in exchange for His worship. From the Gospel of Matthew we read: "Again, the devil taketh him up into an exceeding high mountain, and sheweth him all the kingdoms of the world, and the glory of them; And saith unto him, All these things will I give thee, if thou wilt fall down and worship me" (Matthew 4:8-9). Rather than illegitimately accept the kingdom from anyone but the rightful owner—the Father—Jesus once more repelled the attack: "Then saith Jesus unto him, Get thee hence, Satan: for it is written, Thou shalt worship the Lord thy God, and him only shalt thou serve" (Matthew 4:10). It was then that Satan withdrew after having his attacks successfully repelled three times in a row.

Jesus was set upon again as He was about to undertake our salvation through His substitutionary death on the cross. After telling the apostles that He must go to Jerusalem, suffer, and die, Satan entered Peter and temporarily made him an agent of the enemy. "Then Peter took him, and began to rebuke him, saying, Be it far from thee, Lord: this shall not be unto thee" (Matthew 16:22). As tempting as it was to swallow this enemy propaganda—to avoid torture and death at the hands of the Romans—Jesus resolved to fulfill His divine mission "... and said unto Peter, Get thee behind me, Satan: thou art an offence unto me: for thou savourest not the things that be of God, but those that be of men" (Matthew 16:23). Jesus came into the world for one purpose—to take upon Himself the sins of humanity and to pay for them with His life. Without that selfless act of redemption undertaken by the unblemished Lamb of God, we would all still be captive to sin and prisoners of hell. Jesus' death on the cross opened up those prison cells for all those who believe upon Him.

Let us now study the faithful in Christ to see how they also prevailed when under assault by the enemy. Before obtaining the armor and weapons of the Holy Spirit on the day of Pentecost, the apostles were weak cowards. They could not cast out certain demons—though given the power by Jesus to do so (see Matthew 17:14-21). They feared drowning with Jesus in the boat while crossing the sea (see Matthew 8:23-27). They fled from Jesus in the Garden of Gethsemane upon His arrest (see Matthew 26:47-

56). They did not stand in His defense at either of His trials. Peter (the *Rock* of faith) actually denied three times that he even knew Jesus, when questioned (see Mark 14:66–72). With the exception of John, and a few faithful women (who had nothing to fear of arrest), none of the apostles were present at the crucifixion. Finally, they cowered and hid after Jesus' death, and did not take strength in His promise of resurrection after three days. American General Ulysses S. Grant (1822–1885) astutely observed that "If men make war in slavish obedience to rules, they will fail." Relying upon one's own strength, according to the rules of carnal warfare, cannot possibly succeed in spiritual warfare.

So what transformed these scaredy-cat cowards into roaring-lion victors? The answer can be found on the day of Pentecost: "And suddenly there came a sound from heaven as of a rushing mighty wind, and it filled all the house where they were sitting. And there appeared unto them cloven tongues like as of fire, and it sat upon each of them. And they were all filled with the Holy Ghost, and began to speak with other tongues, as the Spirit gave them utterance" (Acts 2:2–4). Once the armaments of the Holy Spirit were bestowed upon believers as a type of military Defense Support Program, the apostles and disciples were fully equipped for battle against the forces of satanic worldliness.

Peter, who once pleaded to Jesus in weakness "Depart from me; for I am a sinful man, O Lord" (Luke 5:8), became the leader of the apostles through the empowerment of the Holy Spirit and was the first one to preach Christ resurrected to the crowds on Pentecost (see Acts 2:14–35). That sermon converted three thousand souls in a single day. That same Peter, who had fearfully denied knowing Jesus three times, became the same man who boldly stood up to the Sanhedrin and was arrested for it. Defying their commands to cease preaching Christ resurrected, he and the other apostles were later arrested and beaten. Rather than learning that they grieved, we read: "And they departed from the presence of the council, rejoicing that they were counted worthy to suffer shame for his name" (Acts 5:41). Also, empowered by the Holy Spirit of truth, Peter saw through the deceit of Ananias' and Sapphira's outward show of generosity and self-promotion as the work of the devil. He called them out on it, and they fell dead before his feet (see Acts 5:1–11).

Paul and Silas were imprisoned and beaten for exorcising a woman possessed by an evil spirit of divination. Instead of surrendering their faith to adversity, we find them praying in prison and actually singing praises to God (Acts 16:25). Despite the doors of the prison being miraculously opened, they refused to escape, choosing instead to stand fast in their convictions and face the consequences. Paul summarizes the many persecutions he suffered for preaching the gospel while yet never wavering in faith after putting on the full armor of God.

> Of the Jews five times received I forty *stripes* save one. Thrice was I beaten with rods, once was I stoned, thrice I suffered shipwreck, a night and a day I have been in the deep; *In* journeyings often, *in* perils of waters, *in* perils of robbers, *in* perils by *mine own* countrymen, *in* perils by the heathen, *in* perils in the city, *in* perils in the wilderness, *in* perils in the sea, *in* perils among false brethren. (2 Corinthians 11:24–26)

The armor of God and the sword of the Spirit enabled him to achieve these military victories over the successfully executed battle plans of the enemy.

It should be noted here that victory is not limited to the preservation of one's life. "For what shall it profit a man, if he shall gain the whole world, and lose his own soul?" (Mark 8:36). Victory, instead, is also defined by retaining the faith, even under the most vicious and fatal onslaught, thereby holding the spiritual ground unto death and preserving the eternal soul for heaven, to the glory of God and Christ.

We see the first Christian martyrdom victory with the stoning of Stephen. Under the fiercest hostility of the Sanhedrin, Stephen maintained his battle composure and stood firmly: "But he, being full of the Holy Ghost, looked up stedfastly into heaven, and saw the glory of God, and Jesus standing on the right hand of God" (Acts 7:55). His armor was fortified at the time of his greatest trial by knowing that he would soon be with Jesus, who looked down approvingly at his strong defense of the faith.

James, the brother of John, was the first apostle martyred for his Christian faith. The two brothers were known as Boanerges, the *sons of thunder,* so it is likely that James boldly denounced the Romans in preaching the gospel of Christ—for his manner of execution was beheading by the sword, whereas Jewish law dictated execution by stoning for blasphemy (see Leviticus 24:16).

We've seen the enduring power of the armor of God exhibited through the ages, starting with the courage and fortitude displayed by the early Christians against their own Jewish hierarchy; continuing through the Roman persecutions in the arenas—when Christians were fed to the lions and bears for entertainment; through the burning of later Christians at the stake by misguided zealots of the Inquisition period; down to date with Christians being executed as "infidels" in the Middle East for their faith. The enduring lesson through all this is that being girded with the full armor of God will preserve you through the most vigorous assaults of the enemy. His fiery furnaces of persecution will never bring believers to yield or surrender, so that "the princes, governors, and captains, and the king's counsellers, being gathered together, saw these men, upon whose bodies the fire had no power, nor was an hair of their head singed, neither were their coats changed, nor the smell of fire had passed on them" (Daniel 3:27). The almighty power of God can conquer any opposition if only we draw upon it.

8

Anticipate the Attack

Prime Minister of France during WWI, Georges Clemenceau (1841–1929), once stated: "I don't know whether war is an interlude during peace, or peace an interlude during war." For Christians, it is the latter. While we live in bodies of carnal, corrupting flesh, there is never any relief from Satan's perpetual siege against the soul to bring us into submission. There are, however, interludes of peace from his open warfare. If we are truly spiritual beings in Christ, those interludes are short-lived. While Satan targets us all to achieve surrender to the world and to the ways of sin, only those who succumb and join his camp will find lengthy interludes of peace, for "... if Satan rise up against himself, and be divided, he cannot stand, but hath an end" (Mark 3:26). Matthew Henry noted that "A natural state is a dark state, and those who continue in that state meet with no disturbance from Satan and the world but a state of grace is a state of light, and therefore the powers of darkness will violently oppose it."[38] Therefore, if we should ever feel in our lives that war is only a short interlude during peace, then we are actually in the greatest danger of conforming to the ways of the carnal world by neglecting our spiritual souls. The soul not under continuing assault is the soul that has already surrendered to, or made peace with, the enemy. No peace should ever be sought, however, with an enemy relentlessly bent on our destruction. The best defense against that undying malice during this long war for our souls is to anticipate the attack and be ready for it, because the chances of it coming to soldiers who have made peace with God through Christ are 100 percent.

Sun Tzu noted that "The art of war teaches us to rely not on

---

38 Henry, *Commentary*. Vol. 6, 754.

the likelihood of the enemy's not coming, but on our own readiness to receive him; not on the chance of his not attacking, but rather on the fact that we have made our position unassailable" (ch.VIII, ss.11). To make our position impregnable, it is necessary to build fortifications of deterrence—to resist the devil so that he flees—and bulwarks of expectation for the inevitable assault; for it should never be forgotten that the Christian is a soldier living in a war zone. Battle can come at any time—most likely when we least expect it and our guard is down.

We can prepare, in part, by reviewing the history of those already caught unawares and determine the decisive point in their battles which allowed Satan's advance guard to facilitate his offensive incursion, so that we can develop a flexible response to those same situations in our lives, and beat them back. We need not repeat the same mistakes of others, as recorded throughout history. Instead, we need to "Be sober, be vigilant; because your adversary the devil, as a roaring lion, walketh about, seeking whom he may devour" (1 Peter 5:8). Let us be as the watchman in Isaiah: "And he cried, A lion: My lord, I stand continually upon the watchtower in the daytime, and I am set in my ward whole nights" (Isaiah 21:8). Let us never allow the guard tower of our souls to be without a constant sentinel in the turret to alert us of any possible clandestine assault. Let us be ready to repel all attempted infiltrations, however covert. Let us be on our guard especially against Satan's night combat, when our world is without light, and he seeks to gain a tactical advantage through fear, anxiety, and our isolation from others during the long darkness of the night.

We see the very first instance of stealthy subversive warfare in the Garden of Eden, where an eternity of blissful peace seemed a guaranteed prospect to the inhabitants. Yet, in their comfort and ease, Adam and Eve were deceitfully presented with a gift of wisdom by the serpent (Satan) who had covertly infiltrated the garden. He enticed them to disobey God through a two-front assault—an appeal to their eye of flesh, as well as an appeal to their pride of spirit to be equal with God. "And when the woman saw that the tree *was* good for food, and that it *was* pleasant to the eyes, and a tree to be desired to make *one* wise, she took of the fruit thereof, and did eat, and gave also unto her husband with her; and he did eat" (Genesis 3:6). Allowing this successful penetration of their only protective defense (obedience to God) resulted in the entrance of sin into the world, and their expulsion from bliss. Instead of parleying with the enemy, they should have stood their ground and obeyed the only lawful general order given them—"And the LORD God commanded the man, saying, Of every tree of the garden thou mayest freely eat: But of the tree of the knowledge of good and evil, thou shalt not eat of it: for in the day that thou eatest thereof thou shalt surely die" (Genesis 2:16-17). Humanity has been paying the price ever since for that dereliction in the performance of their duty, through lives of toil, pain, and death.

*

Other examples include Nadab and Abihu, who were the two eldest sons of Aaron, the first High Priest of Israel. As members of the newly established priestly order, their duty was to assist the High Priest in *preparing* all offerings made on behalf of the people to God. Only the High Priest himself, though, was allowed to *present* the sacrifices. Yet, in a moment of drunkenness, Nadab and Abihu's guard was penetrated so that the devil was able to sow seeds of prideful familiarity within them. The limitations of their sacred duties were willingly forsaken. Feeling superior to the other Israelites in their preferred positions as priests to God, and also feeling equal now to the High Priest, "... Nadab and Abihu, the sons of Aaron, took either of them his censer, and put fire therein, and put incense thereon, and offered strange fire before the LORD, which he commanded them not" (Leviticus 10:1). As a result of their bold impudence and arrogant sacrilege, "... there went out fire from the LORD, and devoured" (Leviticus 10:2). They fell dead on the spot. For them, judgment was immediately fatal. For many of us, who also allow the enemy to sway us in moments of weakness, judgment can entail a long-term, continued suffering instead. Matthew Henry observed that "Drunken porters keep open gates."[39] Many a fortress has been conquered through those open gates which allow Satan to march

---

39 Henry, *Commentary*. Vol. 1, 59.

Anticipate the Attack

in unopposed, for when the wine is in, the wit is out—as the old proverb warns. Alcohol (and drug) abuse strips away the protective armor of God by putting reason and conscience to sleep.

*

Miriam was Moses' sister and a prophetess of the Lord. She and her brother, Aaron, were appointed by God to assist Moses in his divine commission as leader of Israel, to deliver them from the bondage of Egypt. When Moses married an outsider—an Ethiopian woman—Miriam succumbed to the sins of jealousy, pride, and fear. In that instant, when her guard was down, Satan immediately seized the opportunity to sow evil in her heart. She became jealous that Moses had chosen another woman to be his close confidante. She was prideful in her Jewish heritage as being superior to the Ethiopian's. And she became fearful that she may be replaced in her exalted position by another woman—with Moses favoring his new wife over his sister. Though her position had been previously unassailable by defending Moses, she doubted in God's trust and thereby exposed herself to the enemy's poisoned arrows of dissent which struck her through the heart. That venom of insurrection caused a festering which could not be contained and finally forced itself out, despite the admonition in Psalm 141:3: "Set a watch, O LORD, before my mouth; keep the door of my lips." In an unguarded moment, Miriam first recruited her brother Aaron, and then spewed a sarcastic rejection of Moses' authority. "And Miriam and Aaron spake against Moses because of the Ethiopian woman whom he had married: for he had married an Ethiopian woman" (Numbers 12:1). Through her toxic words, she sowed division amongst her family, and discontent amongst Israel for God's chosen ambassador, Moses. For this treason, she earned God's rebuke. Though Aaron immediately repented, Miriam did not. "And the cloud departed from off the tabernacle; and, behold, Miriam *became* leprous, *white* as snow: and Aaron looked upon Miriam, and, behold, *she was* leprous" (Numbers 12:10). Leprosy was a death penalty. Fortunately for her, Moses interceded on her behalf (just as Jesus unceasingly intercedes for us) and the leprosy sentence was revoked after seven days.

83

*

Twelve spies (rulers representing each of the twelve tribes of Israel) were sent by Moses to search out the land of Canaan ahead of them. They were to take note of the people, their military fortifications, and the land itself for its bounty. Of the twelve men sent, only two of them were properly girded in the full armor of God before departure. Joshua and Caleb kept in mind all of the recent miraculous deliverances of Israel from the Egyptians. They did not forget the overwhelming displays of their all-powerful God in those victories. Their spiritual position was unassailable as they went ahead in unconquerable courage—confident of God's continued protection—fully expecting to dwell in the land of milk and honey promised them by God. The other ten men, however, quickly forgot all that they had seen and experienced of God's omnipotence. They were weak in faith—not properly girded for spiritual warfare—and therefore vulnerable to Satan's deceit because they did not expect his assault on their presumed courage in themselves. They proceeded into enemy territory without having affixed the helmet of hope in God's recent salvation, nor did they wear the breastplate of God's righteousness to guard their hearts. When they saw the enemy soldiers—sons of Anak—as giants, and themselves as grasshoppers in comparison, and then viewed the enemy's mighty walled fortresses, they became faint-hearted through fear and doubt. Their timidity resulted in total personal surrender and an attempt to disarm others of their faith and courage by convincing them also that the mission was lost, saying:

> We be not able to go up against the people; for they *are* stronger than we. And they brought up an evil report of the land which they had searched unto the children of Israel, saying, The land, through which we have gone to search it, *is* a land that eateth up the inhabitants thereof; and all the people that we saw in it *are* men of a great stature.
> (Numbers 13:31–32)

The people then became disheartened by ungirding their own spiritual battle armor and letting it fall to the ground where it lay useless. They, too, surrendered to the same fear of the enemy in despair. They rebelled, planned a hasty retreat back to Egypt—the land of their slavery—and prepared to stone Moses and Aaron to death.

In the United States military, 10 U.S. Code § 899 - Art. 99 partially defines misbehavior before the enemy as:

> Any member of the armed forces who before or in the presence of the enemy ... is guilty of cowardly conduct ... causes false alarms in any command, unit, or place under control of the armed forces ... willfully fails to do his utmost to encounter, engage, capture, or destroy any enemy troops, combatants, vessels, aircraft, or any other thing, which it is his duty so to encounter, engage, capture, or destroy ... shall be punished by death or such other punishment as a court-martial may direct.[40]

For that lack of faith and cowardice in the face of the enemy, and for encouraging the people of Israel to abandon their divinely appointed mission as well, they were sentenced to death by God; "Even those men that did bring up the evil report upon the land, died by the plague before the LORD" (Numbers 14:37). Fear of disobeying the commands of the Lord once again filled the rank and file; trust in His omnipotence was restored; and the optimism of Joshua and Caleb gave them the courage to commit to a course of action toward the military conquest of Canaan.

*

Another instance of mass surrender to the enemy occurred while Moses was up on Mount Sinai receiving the full Levitical Law from God—which included the Ten Commandments. He was up on the mountain for nearly six weeks—"forty days and forty nights" (Exodus 24:18). In his absence, the Israelites became in-

---

40 Legal Information Institute, *10 U.S. Code § 899 - Art. 99 Misbehavior before the enemy*, accessed February 24, 2018, https://www.law.cornell.edu/uscode/text/10/899

different and did not anticipate any imminent danger. It was then that Satan was able to sow seeds of restlessness, impatience, and ingratitude within many of them. Satan distracted them from God's recent glories, and made them unmindful of Moses' role in them as God's chosen vessel of deliverance. They had forgotten all that God had just done for them in their release from 400 years of Egyptian bondage. Forgotten were the ten plagues Moses had inflicted upon Egypt as an absolute demonstration of God's omnipotence against the most powerful man in the Middle East. They even forgot how God (also through Moses) had parted the Red Sea for them to escape through, while drowning Pharaoh's pursuing army in it. Instead, they grumbled for a new god. "And when the people saw that Moses delayed to come down out of the mount, the people gathered themselves together unto Aaron, and said unto him, Up, make us gods, which shall go before us; for *as for* this Moses, the man that brought us up out of the land of Egypt, we wot not what is become of him" (Exodus 32:1). In their idleness, under Satan's influence, they developed a desire for revelry, and demanded a false idol to worship. Their actions, in fact, violated the very *first* of the commandments Moses was currently receiving from God: "I *am* the LORD thy God, which have brought thee out of the land of Egypt, out of the house of bondage. Thou shalt have no other gods before me" (Exodus 20:2-3). This shows that not only is Satan a deceiver, but he is also a mocker. As a result of their idolatry, three thousand men were put to the sword by the faithful Levites. In idleness, we can especially anticipate an attack. The still waters of the pond are breeding grounds for scum. Idle hands are truly the devil's workshop, as the old adage warns. (See also Proverbs 16:27.)

*

In answer to his mother's prayers for a son (for she was childless), Samson was to be a Nazarite and dedicated to the Lord upon his birth. Though the vows of later Nazarites were only for a period of time (see the example of Paul in Acts 18:18), Samson's were for life. As one of Israel's judges, he began to deliver them from the oppressive Philistines—a work completed subsequently by Samuel, Saul, and especially David. Part of Samson's Nazarite vows included that no razor should ever touch upon his head. As his hair grew in length over the years, his physical strength became superhuman.

Though Samson's dedication to the Lord should have kept him from danger, he often veered away from the path of holiness by lusting after strange women. One such woman, a harlot of the Philistines, was his downfall. In unguarded moments, we do not anticipate the eyes becoming the inlets of sin. But physical lust knows no other way in, and Satan will force his assault any way possible at every opportunity, through any breach discovered in our defenses. Samson succumbed to desire for Delilah—a woman who was secretly paid to discover his weakness and betray him to the Philistines. After being seduced by Delilah to reveal the source of his strength, he was undone. "And when Delilah saw that he had told her all his heart, she sent and called for the lords of the Philistines ... [who] took him, and put out his eyes, and brought him down to Gaza, and bound him with fetters of brass; and he did grind in the prison house" (Judges 16:18–21). It is somewhat fitting that Samson's eyes, the inroads of lust, were put out by the Philistines. In doing so, however, they unwittingly sealed up that breach in Samson's armor so that when his hair grew back, and he re-dedicated himself to the Lord, his superhuman strength returned. After being brought up from the prisons to be mocked by the Philistines during a festival for their false god, Samson was given one final opportunity to begin Israel's deliverance. While claiming that he needed to lean on the columns for support, instead, he pushed them apart and brought down the entire structure, killing all in attendance, including himself.

*

Saul was the first king of Israel. Facing an invading army of Philistines, he was instructed to wait for Samuel the prophet to return on the seventh day in order to offer sacrifices to the Lord for their victory. Saul did not anticipate that his character was being tested—to see if he truly was an obedient man after God's own heart as king over Israel. Nor did he anticipate the results the satanic exploitation of ambition and impatience would impose upon him and his descendants. His new-found ambition brought about a desire to rule over Israel with absolute power in both civil and sacred things, despite his necessary subservience to God and His prophet Samuel. His impatience led him to acting as his own priest in defiance of God's order for him to await Samuel's return. "And Saul said, Bring hither a burnt offering to me, and peace offerings. And he offered the burnt offering" (1 Samuel 13:9). In this moment of vulnerability, Satan acted upon Saul's heart, inspiring him to act rashly and foolishly. The results were that he and his heirs were rejected by God for the kingly lineage. "But now thy kingdom shall not continue: the LORD hath sought him a man after his own heart, and the LORD hath commanded him *to be* captain over his people, because thou hast not kept *that* which the LORD commanded thee" (1 Samuel 13:14). His kingdom was forfeited in favor of another family line—that of David—because he did not anticipate Satan's attack upon his character.

*

Though David was considered the greatest king of Israel because he was a man after God's own heart, and therein obtained great military victories for Israel, he nevertheless was also caught off guard—unmindful of the devil's relentless desire to impose sinful temptations. As a result, he yielded to a moment of lust in his idleness, which eventually led to murder. He should have been with his men on the battlefield, "But David tarried still at Jerusalem. And it came to pass in an eveningtide, that David arose from off his bed, and walked upon the roof of the king's house: and from the roof he saw a woman washing herself; and the woman *was* very beautiful to look upon" (2 Samuel 11:1-2). David succumbed to lust for Bathsheba, and acted upon that lust with her. When she became pregnant with his child, he plotted to conceal their sin. He ordered Bathsheba's husband, Uriah, home from the battlefront so that he might be intimate with his wife. Uriah would then suppose the child to be his own. But Uriah stayed with his men instead and did not go home. It was then, when

Anticipate the Attack

David knew he and Bathsheba would be exposed for their adultery, that he sent a letter to his commander, Joab. In it, Joab was ordered to "Put Uriah out in front where the fighting is fiercest. Then withdraw from him so he will be struck down and die" (2 Samuel 11:15). David compounded his first sin of adultery with a cover-up sin of murder. He should have anticipated Satan's attack, and prepared for it by following the actions of Job who protected himself against lust: "I made a covenant with mine eyes; why then should I think upon a maid?" (Job 31:1). How many murders throughout history have been committed because of lust and adultery?

*

Solomon is acknowledged to be the wisest man in history (except for Jesus). When he ascended to the throne as a young man, he prayed for wisdom to govern his people rather than for riches, power, or prestige. God was so pleased with his humility that He granted Solomon wisdom in measures far beyond that of any person who had ever lived. Yet, despite that vast store of wisdom, he willingly fell into folly by allowing lust into his life through unguarded eyes. "But king Solomon loved many strange women, together with the daughter of Pharaoh, women of the Moabites, Ammonites, Edomites, Zidonians, *and* Hittites" (1 Kings 11:1). It was through these women that Satan gained a foothold in Solomon's life by deceiving him to seek after foreign gods to please his foreign wives, and thereby throw off his allegiance to the one true God. He did not anticipate that his actions would amount to making a personal peace treaty with the enemy during perpetual spiritual war—thereby abandoning the covenant with God. "For it came to pass, when Solomon was old, *that* his wives turned away his heart after other gods: and his heart was not perfect with the LORD his God, as *was* the heart of David his father." (1 Kings 11:4). As a result, God tore the unified kingdom from his son Rehoboam, and gave the greater portion of it (ten tribes) to Jeroboam instead. This marked the historical division between the Kingdom of Judah and the Kingdom of Israel. They were never reunited, and they warred often upon each other until both were eventually conquered individually by heathen armies as a result of their continued idolatries against God.

*

To highlight the subtlety of Satan, we have this example of Elisha and his servant. Because Elisha the prophet was filled with the Spirit of God and presented a formidable fortress for the enemy to assail, Satan instead went after his weaker servant to undermine their work. During Gehazi's service to Elisha, he was eyewitness to many of Elisha's miracles. It would seem to follow that after seeing and believing, Gehazi would also have been an inviolable saint. Witnessing the awesome power of God being demonstrated through Elisha—especially in a miracle of raising the dead—Gehazi, too, should have presented an unassailable stronghold to the enemy. Yet, we'll see how those fortifications were bypassed.

When Naaman the Syrian was healed by Elisha of his leprosy, he glorified God. "Now I know that there is no God in all the world except in Israel. So please accept a gift from your servant" (2 Kings 5:15). Elisha refused the payment, giving credit for the work solely to God. After hearing this verbal exchange between Naaman and Elisha, the trap was set for Gehazi who did not anticipate an attack upon himself—probably feeling safe and secure that his master would always be the intended target instead. Presented by Satan with an opportunity to enrich himself and his posterity, Gehazi yielded the spiritual high ground in succumbing to greed. "But Gehazi, the servant of Elisha the man of God, said, Behold, my master hath spared Naaman this Syrian, in not receiving at his hands that which he brought: but, *as* the LORD liveth, I will run after him, and take somewhat of him" (2 Kings 5:20). He followed after Naaman. When Naaman saw Gehazi in pursuit, he became worried that something might have happened to Elisha. Gehazi removed his fear; "And he said, All *is* well. My master hath sent me, saying, Behold, even now there be come to me from mount Ephraim two young men of the sons of the prophets: give them, I pray thee, a talent of silver, and two changes of garments" (2 Kings 5:22). Gehazi's lie undermined the fledgling faith in Naaman for the God of Israel by misrepresenting Him as unable to supply His own prophets with money or clothes, and having to rely on others to do so. As a prophet of God, Elisha had knowledge of this encounter, though being many miles away at the time. When he confronted Gehazi over the matter, Gehazi compounded his sin with more lies. For this greed and deceit, Elisha pronounced the sentence that Naaman's former leprosy would return upon Gehazi. This failure to expect the enemy's assault resulted in a judgment of perpetual leprosy for Gehazi's posterity as well.

*

We see another example of an unanticipated assault, with greed acting as the conduit through which the enemy's attack succeeded. Judas Iscariot was one of the original apostles, and lived closely with Jesus for years. After hearing the wisdom of His preaching, and seeing firsthand the many miracles that absolutely defy naturalistic explanations, he nevertheless capitulated and compromised his spiritual integrity. It may have been his natural weakness towards the love of money, for we read of Judas' character in John 12:6 "... not that he cared for the poor; but because he was a thief, and had the bag, and bare what was put therein." Why he was allowed by Jesus to carry the money bag for the apostles is uncertain. Maybe it was to provide an opportunity for him to repent and overcome his weakness. If so, it didn't work. When confronted with their sins, people either repent and turn away from them, or they double down on them in self-justifying defense and defiance. This was Judas' chosen course of action.

When the chief priests and scribes of the temple came to Judas seeking his help in betraying Jesus, he asked "... What will ye give me, and I will deliver him unto you? And they covenanted with him for thirty pieces of silver" (Matthew 26:15). Instead of hanging tough on the spiritual battlefield by expecting an assault from the avowed enemies of Christ, Judas willingly surrendered his allegiance to Him. He ended up hanging himself from a tree.

Peter provides us with yet another example of how even the most devout Christians are still vulnerable when they don't anticipate an attack. Peter lived with Jesus for His entire ministry. He became the *de facto* leader of the apostles through his boldness. He witnessed Jesus' miracles and then performed them himself after Jesus had sent the apostles out in pairs to preach throughout Israel. Despite that, he exposed himself to the enemy through overconfidence in his own strength of resolve. From Peter's example we need to glean the following wisdom: "Wherefore let him that thinketh he standeth take heed lest he fall" (1 Corinthians 10:12). Peter swore to Jesus that, even if all had fallen away from Him, he would remain devoted to Jesus even unto death. It was then that Jesus warned Peter of his overconfidence, and that, when confronted by the very real possibility of actually sharing in Jesus' fate, he would falter. Simon (Peter's other name) was even forewarned by Jesus of the imminent attack. "And the Lord said, Simon, Simon, behold, Satan hath desired *to have* you, that he may sift *you* as wheat" (Luke 22:31), so that Peter should have doubled his vigilance. Yet, in his pride, Peter felt secure and neglected the warning. When Jesus was arrested, Peter and the apostles all ran away and abandoned Him. But Peter then returned and stealthily followed behind. It was then that he was confronted by other people in the amassed crowd with having been an accomplice of Jesus. He denied that he was one of Jesus' disciples. Yet again, he was accused, and again he denied it. After the third accusation began to draw more attention to him, Peter completely surrendered to fear. "Then began he to curse and to swear, *saying*, I know not the man" (Matthew 26:74). The rooster then crowed, just as Jesus had prophesied. Peter retreated and wept bitter tears.

*

A more recent example of how a literal lack of expectation for combat leads to battlefield defeat can be seen in the demand for Israel to trade land for peace. In the Bible, it is clearly shown how all of the land in dispute today was irrevocably deeded by God to Israel. The argument that the land belongs to the Palestinians is voided by the fact that God promised the conquered Canaanites' land to Abraham. "God confirmed it at least 55 times with an oath and stated at least 12 times that the covenant was everlasting."[41] The Arab nations (including the so-called Palestinians) sprung from Abraham's son Ishmael (his bastard son by Hagar the Egyptian handmaiden). Therefore it follows that the legitimate heir to the land of Israel is Isaac, (the son of the two married Israelites Abraham and Sarah), and not Ishmael. In fact, when Abraham sought to make Ishmael his heir—"And Abraham said unto God, O that Ishmael might live before thee!" (Genesis 17:18) —God denied the request by stating unequivocally: "Sarah thy wife shall bear thee a son indeed; and thou shalt call his name Isaac: and I will establish my covenant with him for an everlasting covenant, *and* with his seed after him" (Genesis 17:19). The disputed territories of the Gaza Strip and the West Bank are clearly titled to Israel.

After Moses had died, God commanded Joshua: "Moses my servant is dead; now therefore arise, go over this Jordan, thou, and all this people, unto the land which I do give to them, *even* to the children of Israel. Every place that the sole of your foot shall tread upon, that have I given unto you, as I said unto Moses. From the wilderness and this Lebanon even unto the great river, the river Euphrates, all the land of the Hittites, and unto the great sea toward the going down of the sun, shall be your coast" (Joshua 1:2–4). It should be noted that this original deed actually included large parts of Egypt, Syria, Jordan, and Iraq; so to claim that tiny portions within that vast swath of land—the West Bank and the Gaza Strip—are *not* part of Israel is ludicrous. The Golan Heights in Syria, as well as the Egyptian Sinai Peninsula, also became part of that land dispute after war.

When Joshua conquered the Canaanite territories for the freed Hebrews and claimed their real estate inheritance—which God led them to after forty years' punishment of wandering in the Sinai desert—there never were people called Palestinians

---

41 "Boundaries of the Promised Land." Christian Bible Teaching. Accessed March 01, 2018. https://www.differentspirit.org/articles/boundaries.php.

dwelling there. In fact, the Canaanites were Hebrew descendants of Canaan, the son of Ham, the grandson of Noah. Canaan was cursed by Noah as recorded in Genesis 9:25: "Cursed *be* Canaan; a servant of servants shall he be unto his brethren." The conquest of Canaan was therefore a divine judgment upon the wickedness of his descendants. The people occupying Canaan at the time of the conquests constituted seven tribes. None of those nations exists today who might make an ancient claim to the land.

> When the LORD thy God shall bring thee into the land whither thou goest to possess it, and hath cast out many nations before thee, the Hittites, and the Girgashites, and the Amorites, and the Canaanites, and the Perizzites, and the Hivites, and the Jebusites, seven nations greater and mightier than thou; And when the LORD thy God shall deliver them before thee; thou shalt smite them, *and* utterly destroy them; thou shalt make no covenant with them, nor shew mercy unto them: the Canaanites; the Hittites; the Girgashites; the Amorites; the Perizzites; the Hivites; and the Jebusites.
> (Deuteronomy 7:1–2)

In AD 132, a Jew named Simon ben Kosevah—called Simon bar Kokhba—led an insurrection against the Romans. The Roman emperor Hadrian crushed the revolt, and in an effort to wipe the existence of Israel from history, renamed the region as *Syria Palaestina*. This is where the modern notion of a pre-existing nation-state called Palestine originated. It was a land which throughout history has been ruled over by Romans, Islamic and Christian crusaders, Turks, and even the British; it was never an independent entity governed by any people known as *Palestinians*. As such, there is no distinct Palestinian language or Palestinian culture.[42]

Since the reclamation of the nation-state of Israel in the Middle East in 1948, there have been wars between Israel and the surrounding nations. In 1967, Egypt, Jordan, and Syria waged

---

42 Thomas, Harrol, "Why Are Israel and the Palestinian People Always Fighting over Land? Was There Ever Such a Place Called Palestine?" Accessed March 8, 2018. http://www.gracebibletimes.com

war upon Israel. The *Six-Day War* resulted in Arab defeat, and the conquering of the disputed territories from which the Arab nations had strategically launched assaults. According to UN Resolution 242, which guarantees nations "safe and recognized boundaries free from threats or acts of force," Israel kept the conquered territories. It is unknown why Arabs insist on carving up Israel, the smallest nation in that region of the Middle East, to create a Palestinian state when a larger Palestinian nation could be created by Arabs donating small corners of bordering nations such as Lebanon, Syria, and Jordan—other than the fact that their true desire is to destroy Israel entirely.

Political pressure forced the Israelis to give back portions of those lands. Though some did anticipate that these regained territories would yield assault positions to the enemy, the political leadership of the time did not foresee it. As a result of trading "land for peace" all they got was war. Whenever land was surrendered, it was shortly afterwards that rockets were launched into Israel from that surrendered land.

*

The only example we see in the Bible of someone continuously girded in the full armor of God, filled with the Holy Spirit in operational readiness anticipating the assault, was Jesus. He is also the only person in history, not coincidentally, who never succumbed to sin—existing as both God and man. His divinity provided safe haven even behind the lines, deep in enemy territory.

After His baptism, instead of waiting for the inevitable assault, Jesus deployed an advanced force operation by meeting the enemy head-on; "Then was Jesus led up of the Spirit into the wilderness to be tempted of the devil" (Matthew 4:1). It is especially noteworthy to observe that Jesus went to battle under unfavorable HALT (Hungry, Angry, Lonely, Tired) conditions; in this case extreme hunger. "And when he had fasted forty days and forty nights, he was afterward ... [tempted]" (Matthew 4:2) He had no supplies to fortify Him. His only materiel was Scripture, the very Word of God. He wielded the sword of the Spirit and drove off the enemy aggression repeatedly. His battle armor was thoroughly tested in the wilderness, and proven resilient to any attack.

Other HALT conditions (tired, lonely) beset Jesus as He was about to be arrested. First, He prayed to God for strength in the Garden of Gethsemane; "Then saith he unto them, My soul is exceeding sorrowful, even unto death: tarry ye here, and watch with me" (Matthew 26:38). Yet, all the disciples fell asleep and left Jesus to face the imminent engagement alone. He knew of the upcoming decisive victory orchestrated by the enemy against His body that would take His life in a most horrible way through torture and death on the cross. He prayed for fortification to undergo the ordeal and God sent reinforcements; "And there appeared an angel unto him from heaven, strengthening him" (Luke 22:43). Upon His arrest, they all fled from Him, leaving Him truly alone. Girded still in the full armor of God, He was able to complete His mission of redemption on the cross, and break the bondage of sin for those who believe upon Him.

Detect Deceit

It has been said that truth is the first casualty of war—that war causes deceit. In spiritual warfare that model is reversed. It is deceit itself which causes all subsequent casualties. Sun Tzu observed long ago that all warfare was based upon deception, (*ch*.I, *ss*.18). Satan could gain no foothold in our lives were it not for us embracing his lies by forgetting that he "abode not in the truth, because there is no truth in him. When he speaketh a lie, he speaketh of his own: for he is a liar, and the father of it" (John 8:44). He lied to Eve in the very beginning, resulting in a fallen humanity. He has been lying ever since for he is "... the Devil, and Satan, which deceiveth the whole world" (Revelation 12:9). His campaign of deception is perpetual.

The only tried-and-true method of detecting his deceit and avoiding his traps and snares is by running every word, thought, and deed through the filter of Holy Scripture to decrypt the hidden, conflicting messages. It becomes imperative, therefore, to read and study the Word of God; to make the Bible our prism through which everything passes. In that way, we may observe clearly the total spectrum of perceptions and persuasions, identify and discard the deceit, while drinking in the white light of truth as a plant does sunlight, to recharge us spiritually and to fill our arsenal with all manner of scriptural weapons to guard us against that deceit.

We've seen the consequences of failing to anticipate Satan's attack in the previous chapter. Now we'll see through those examples, and various others, the subtlety of deceit precipitating those attacks. As noted above, believing in the first lie ever told, that "Ye shall not surely die" (Genesis 3:4), resulted in humanity being expelled from paradise to live a life of toil, pain, and eventual death. Furthermore, we can see how the slippery slope of sin progresses from one sin into another, and worse, sin. Belief in the lie that we don't really have to offer our best to God fueled the jealousy which resulted in the first murder ever, when "the LORD had respect unto Abel and to his offering: But unto Cain and to his offering he had not respect. And Cain was very wroth, and his countenance fell" (Genesis 4:4–5). Also, believing the lie that hedonism and sexual perversion—exalting the flesh, while forsaking the spiritual holiness of God—led to the fiery destruction of Sodom and Gomorrah. It is a lesson for all time that the wages of sin is death.

We can learn more from other specific examples as well by showing the consequences of disbelieving God's solemn word and accepting the lies of the devil instead. Although Abraham and Sarah were promised their *own* son (Isaac) by God, they both swallowed Satan's lie that she would be barren because of her advanced age. "And Sarai said unto Abram, Behold now, the LORD hath restrained me from bearing: I pray thee, go in unto my maid; it may be that I may obtain children by her. And Abram hearkened to the voice of Sarai" (Genesis 16:2). This faithless action resulted in the birth of Ishmael, the father of the Arab nation, of which many Muslim members are at perpetual war with Israel (the children of Isaac) to this day.

Belief in Satan's lie that his hunger would result in death by starvation—ignoring God's promise in Scripture that "Every moving thing that liveth shall be meat for you; even as the green herb have I given you all things" (Genesis 9:3)—led Esau to sell his birthright to Jacob for a bowl of stew. Did not Abraham acknowledge in Genesis 22 that the Lord will provide?

After 400 years of the Israelites being enslaved by the Egyptians, God promised to Moses "And I am come down to deliver them out of the hand of the Egyptians, and to bring them up out of that land unto a good land and a large, unto a land flowing with milk and honey" (Exodus 3:8). Despite this promise, as soon as the Israelites were freed and found themselves in the desert, they believed Satan's lies that Moses was leading them to their death by starvation in the desert. The miracle of God's provision of heavenly manna should have fortified them against Satan's deceit, yet they believed the lie that it was not sufficient to sustain them. They confronted Moses: "Who shall give us flesh to eat?" (Numbers 11:4). As a result, God sent numerous quail. "And while the flesh *was* yet between their teeth, ere it was chewed, the wrath of the LORD was kindled against the people, and the LORD smote the people with a very great plague" (Numbers 11:33). The deceit that manna, the bread of life, was insufficient for them was their undoing.

The persisting belief in false gods by the Israelites was a constant thorn in their sides planted by Satan. God had revealed Himself plainly to them through the most astounding miracles, yet they persisted in believing the lie that other gods existed. When Moses went up the mountain to receive the Law from God, he was gone for forty days and nights. In his absence, the people believed the devil's lie that he was forever gone and that they were left alone without any God. They embraced that apostasy by throwing off their allegiance to the one true God, and created their own false god to worship in the form of a golden calf. The consequences of that rebellion immediately cost the lives of three thousand men at the foot of Mount Sinai.

We see that familiar pattern repeated throughout Scripture. Belief in the devil's lie that Nadab and Abihu (the sons of Aaron) were equal to their father the High Priest led to their death by holy fire. Miriam's acceptance of the lie that she was equal to Moses in God's eye led to her leprosy. The ten spies who could not perceive the deceit of Satan in believing that the Canaanites were too strong for the Israelites to conquer—despite God being at the head of their army—led to the forty-year wandering exile in the desert until all of that faithless generation had died off. Korah's rebellion in embracing the deceit that he and all of the other 250 elders and princes were equal to Moses and Aaron in authority—despite God singling out those two specifically—led to their destruction as well. Even Moses and Aaron were eventually deceived into forgetting that *the Lord* worked through them, by assuming the authority upon themselves; "And Moses and Aaron gathered the congregation together before the rock, and he said unto them, Hear now, ye rebels; must we fetch you water out of this rock?" (Numbers 20:10). Their bold usurpation of omnipotence in stating that "we" fetch the water, brought upon them the Lord's judgment: "And the LORD spake unto Moses and Aaron, Because ye believed me not, to sanctify me in the eyes of the children of Israel, therefore ye shall not bring this congregation into the land which I have given them" (Numbers 20:12). Moses and Aaron never set foot in the Promised Land.

We see further examples of Satan's deceit causing the fall of many, even after the Israelites had come into their Promised Land. Samson was dedicated to God at birth to be a *Nazarite*— one separated unto God. As a sign of this devotion, no razor could touch upon his head. Samson performed many feats of great strength against the enemy Philistines. Yet, he took that strength for granted and allowed himself to be deceived by one of Satan's agents, Delilah, into thinking that she loved him. He unwisely revealed to her that his uncut hair was the source of his strength. While he slept, she cut it off. Samson lost his superhuman strength, was captured, blinded, and made a slave. After his hair grew back, he died through one last physical effort in bringing down the Philistine palace.

King Saul was deceived when he believed the lie that Samuel was not returning. Saul then offered the sacrifice in Samuel's place, though he was specifically ordered to await Samuel's return on the seventh day. His impatience in offering the sacrifice early on the seventh day—just before Samuel's return—forfeited the descent of kings through his family line.

King David believed the lie that it was the number of his armed forces which had guaranteed Israel's victories, rather than the Lord God's almighty power. He succumbed to earthly pride in earthly strength; "And Satan stood up against Israel, and provoked David to number Israel" (1 Chronicles 21:1). He took a census of the people so that he could boast of their great numbers. That action brought upon Israel a great plague as punishment which killed seventy thousand men.

King Solomon believed the lie that it was OK to marry foreign wives and appease them by building altars to their false gods— despite the First Commandment to have no other gods but the

God of Israel. That deceit led to the division of Israel into two separate warring kingdoms.

Gehazi, the servant of Elisha the prophet, was deceived into thinking that his secret dealings with Naaman the Syrian would go undetected by the Holy Spirit of God. Embracing that deceit brought a curse of leprosy upon him and his family.

Another danger of undetected deceit can be seen through the secret sins in our own lives that we've allowed to creep in, under the guise that they are not really big sins. Getting comfortable with sins in our lives—no matter how small they may seem to us—is what holds open the door for greater sins to enter. Little "white lies" become greater lies until the truth is lost and forgotten, just as one uncultivated weed can eventually choke out an entire garden with overgrowth. We see this happening through Israel's constant backsliding into sins of complacency in worship, in allowing false doctrine to supersede Scripture, and in offerings of lesser quality, etc., which eventually cost them their kingdoms under the Assyrian, Babylonian, and Roman conquests as divine punishment.

In the New Testament, we see the glaring examples of Judas Iscariot falling for the deceit of Satan—that by delivering the Lord to His enemies, Jesus could prove Himself to be the Messiah and thereby free Israel from Roman rule as Israel's new King. Yet, Jesus did not come to rule physically, but to rule spiritually in our souls by dying in our place with our sins upon Him so as to redeem us and reconcile sinful humanity with holy God. When He was condemned by the Sanhedrin instead—just as Scripture foretold He would be—Judas hanged himself in remorse. And we see the rejection of the true Messiah by the greater part of Israel, under the guidance of the Jewish elders, priests, and scribes of the Sanhedrin who swallowed Satan's lie that Jesus was just another false prophet. That renunciation resulted in the destruction of the Temple forty years later, and the final conquest of Israel by the Roman army not too many more years after that. Israel as a peopled nation was ended and scattered worldwide until the modern establishment of the State of Israel in 1948.

Jesus warned of specific deceit to be on guard against: "And Jesus answered and said unto them, Take heed that no man deceive you. For many shall come in my name, saying, I am Christ; and shall deceive many" (Matthew 24:4-5). Josephus makes note of several false prophets that rose to some prominence after Jesus' death and resurrection such as Theudas, Menahem, and Simon bar Giora, who led many people to their deaths through insurrection against Rome. Simon Magus was another type of false Messiah whom the people claimed to be "the great power of God" (Acts 8:10), as was Dositheus the Samaritan.

In our time, we've seen false Messiahs such as Charles Manson, who convinced some gullible people that he was Jesus Christ returned. Under his orders, followers known as the *Manson Family* committed some of the most atrocious acts of murder and butchery in criminal history. Seventy followers of David Koresh, the leader of the Branch Davidians, were killed alongside him in a shoot-out with the federal government, deceived by the lie that Koresh—an alleged sexual and child abuser—was a prophet of God, and father of the returning Messiah. Religious cult leader Jim Jones was responsible for the mass suicide and murder of over 900 followers, including 304 children. Some willingly, others forcefully, drank cyanide-laced Kool-aid. Marshall Applewhite, founder of the Heaven's Gate religious cult, convinced thirty-nine members of his group to commit suicide in order to graduate from the Human Evolutionary Level. They were deceived into believing that their souls would reach an extraterrestrial spacecraft following the comet Hale-Bopp.

All of those listed above, as well as numerous others throughout history too lengthy to detail, could have been spared the tragic consequences of their actions had they first detected the deceit that led them to their catastrophic actions. In each instance, a healthy understanding of Scripture—God's promises and warnings—would have averted disaster. But because they were not armed with the truth, they could not detect Satan's deceit and, instead, followed the extreme unscriptural doctrines promoted by his agents. History records them all as abject lessons of evil for us to learn from.

10

Identify Satan's Allies

It is not enough to identify Satan's planted lies and deceit that germinate within us through our own ignorance and unguarded temptations; we must also be on our guard against the assault coming from without—especially through those close to us we may not even suspect. Jesus warned us to be vigilant against these covert cell groups; "... a man's foes *shall be* they of his own household" (Matthew 10:36). He further elaborated: "For from henceforth there shall be five in one house divided, three against two, and two against three. The father shall be divided against the son, and the son against the father; the mother against the daughter, and the daughter against the mother; the mother in law against her daughter in law, and the daughter in law against her mother in law" (Luke 12:52-53). This division is especially observable in the current American political scene in which families and friends have been broken apart over several recent election results. Yet, the immediate political battle is merely another manifestation of the eternal spiritual battle. (See Chapter Fifteen for a more in-depth analysis on politics.)

Just as the ancient military proverb states that *the enemy of my enemy is my friend*, in spiritual warfare, the reverse is also true; *the friend of my enemy is my enemy*. Satan has many devout allies in this world, and many more who are unwittingly duped into being so. We must therefore be on our constant guard against his secret agents in all their guises with their destructive propaganda. A study in biblical examples will again help us gain some perspective and insight into how to identify those acting as agents of evil.

In the beginning of humanity, we see Satan employing deception to create his first ally. Though Adam and Eve were forbidden to eat the fruit of the tree of the knowledge of good and evil, Satan first persuaded Eve to join his rebellious cause against God, who in turn then recruited Adam. "[S]he took of the fruit thereof, and did eat, and gave also unto her husband with her; and he did eat" (Genesis 3:6). Allying with Satan in defying God's command resulted in their expulsion from the Garden, and the fall of all subsequent humanity into a state of sin. Their fateful choice replaced ease and eternal bliss with toil and death.

After Abel's brother, Cain, had become an agent of fratricidal evil and murdered Abel in a jealous rage, the corruption of Cain and his progeny—Satan's allies—spread throughout humanity to the point where "the wickedness of man *was* great in the earth, and *that* every imagination of the thoughts of his heart *was* only evil continually" (Genesis 6:5). The punishment for that apostasy was the cleansing of the earth through a global flood in Noah's day.

Happily for Lot, he was warned by God's angels of Satan's allies in Sodom and Gomorrah and instructed to leave that sinful region. Just after he did, "the LORD rained upon Sodom and upon Gomorrah brimstone and fire from the LORD out of heaven; And he overthrew those cities, and all the plain, and all the inhabitants of the cities, and that which grew upon the ground" (Genesis 19:24–25). Through sinful lifestyles we, too, may identify those slated for destruction so as to avoid confederacy with them and escape the consequences of their punishment, just as Lot did.

Although Joseph's brothers, in their jealousy, acted as agents of the enemy when they "... sold Joseph to the Ishmeelites for twenty *pieces* of silver: and they brought Joseph into Egypt" (Genesis 37:28), God used that situation to save Israel during a severe seven-year famine. Joseph finally revealed to his brothers that "...God did send me before you to preserve life" (Genesis 45:5). Though God had allowed Joseph's brothers to act as temporary enemy agents in this particular situation, it was God's all-knowing plan for the better good.

Another example of a man allying himself with Satan against his own brother occurred at Mount Sinai while Moses was up on the mountain receiving the Law from God. Though Aaron was appointed by God to assist Moses in the freeing of Israel from Egyptian bondage and in leading the Israelites to the Promised Land, he succumbed to Satan's guile and became an ally in directing the construction of the golden calf for idolatrous worship in Moses' absence. "And the LORD was very angry with Aaron to have destroyed him" (Deuteronomy 9:20). Were it not for Moses' intercessory prayer providing a sort of covering fire for Aaron to escape immediate judgment, he, too, would have been destroyed alongside the three thousand idolatrous Israelites who were put to the sword that day.

God had repeatedly commanded Israel not to intermarry with His enemies; "For they will turn away thy son from following me, that they may serve other gods: so will the anger of the LORD be kindled against you, and destroy thee suddenly" (Deuteronomy 7:4). Yet Israel disobeyed and often allied themselves with Satan's minions—the daughters of Moab in this biblical instance. As expected, it wasn't long before they corrupted Israel. "And they called the people unto the sacrifices of their gods: and the people did eat, and bowed down to their gods" (Numbers 25:2). For this idolatrous treason, God commanded that the leaders in the rebellion be immediately hanged, while twenty-four thousand idolatrous Israelites died subsequently through a punishing plague sent by God.

One man's betrayal may bring defeat to an entire army. Though God had commanded His people not to take any spoils from their battle at Jericho, "... Achan, the son of Carmi, the son of Zabdi, the son of Zerah, of the tribe of Judah, took of the accursed thing: and the anger of the LORD was kindled against the children of Israel" (Joshua 7:1). For allying themselves against God in embracing that which He declared accursed beforehand, God abandoned Israel in their military conquests. Their next battle—which should have been an easy conquest—resulted in a humiliating defeat and retreat. It wasn't until the sin was uncovered and the transgressor punished, that God resumed His position as Commander-in-Chief, and the military victories continued.

Military victory was only possible when the Israelites honored their covenant with God. Unfortunately, they were often deceived by the propaganda of enemy agents into breaking that alliance and siding with the enemy. "And they forsook the LORD, and served Baal and Ashtaroth" (Judges 2:13). Because they were oath-breakers, "... the anger of the LORD was hot against Israel, and he delivered them into the hands of spoilers that spoiled them, and he sold them into the hands of their enemies round about, so that they could not any longer stand before their enemies" (Judges 2:14). When they repented, God appointed certain people to be Judges over Israel to deliver them from their current travails—the most notable example being Samson, who yet failed to detect Delilah as an ally of the enemy, which led to his own downfall.

We see, from Judges 19, an especially egregious example of what Satan's allies are capable of in starting a war within the tribes of Israel. As a man and his concubine were traveling, they decided to lodge for the night in Gibeah, a city of the tribe of Benjamin. "*Now* as they were making their hearts merry, behold, the men of the city, certain sons of Belial, beset the house round about, *and* beat at the door, and spake to the master of the house, the old man, saying, Bring forth the man that came into thine house, that we may know him [carnally]" (Judges 19:22). The master of the house would not allow these agents of the enemy to sodomize the man. Thwarted at that effort, they took, instead, his concubine and abused her all night long. At dawn, she tried to return unto the house, but died on the doorstep. This abuse caused the other tribes of Israel to demand justice by having the tribe of Benjamin surrender the Gibeah perpetrators. Benjamin refused. The ensuing war with the other eleven tribes of Israel killed tens of thousands of Israelites, and nearly extinguished the tribe of Benjamin.

Eli the priest was a righteous man who had judged Israel for forty years. Unfortunately, "... the sons of Eli *were* sons of Belial; they knew not the LORD" (1 Samuel 2:12). Having allied themselves with Satan and his evil ways, they brought shame and dishonor upon the holy priesthood. Though Eli knew of his sons' wickedness, he became accomplice to their treason against God by not reproving them for it and removing them from office. He therefore earned God's judgment for loving his sons more than the Lord. "For I have told him that I will judge his house for ever for the iniquity which he knoweth; because his sons made themselves vile, and he restrained them not. And therefore I have sworn unto the house of Eli, that the iniquity of Eli's house shall not be purged with sacrifice nor offering for ever" (1 Samuel 3:13-14). Despite the awareness that his own children had become agents of the enemy, Eli allowed their infiltration of the priesthood. The judge was now to be judged in the Divine court of justice. His sentence was death to him and his sons, and the high office of priesthood forever stripped from his descendants. Shortly after the prophetic sentence was passed, both of his sons died in battle, routed by the Philistines. When Eli heard the news of his sons' deaths, and of the capture of the Holy Ark of the Covenant by the Philistines, he fell backwards off his chair, broke his neck, and died on the spot. His life became forfeit because he failed to perceive that his own children—with whom he was allied—had become Satan's allies.

Before David became king, he faithfully served King Saul. He killed the Philistine giant Goliath in combat. He led Israel's armies to victory after victory. It became a known saying that though Saul had killed thousands of Israel's enemies, David had killed tens of thousands. When Saul heard this, he became filled with a murderous jealousy, which consumed his soul. Though David trusted Saul as his king and benefactor, Saul had become Satan's ally, obsessed with murdering him. "And Saul spake to Jonathan his son, and to all his servants, that they should kill David" (1 Samuel 19:1). As Satan's ally, Saul's hatred was also expressed towards the priests of God who had assisted David during his flight from Saul;

> And the king said to Doeg, Turn thou, and fall upon the priests. And Doeg the Edomite turned, and he fell upon the priests, and slew on that day fourscore and five persons that did wear a linen ephod. And Nob, the city of the priests, smote he with the edge of the sword, both men and women, children and sucklings, and oxen, and asses, and sheep, with the edge of the sword.
> (1 Samuel 22:18-19)

David spent much time during Saul's remaining years fleeing from him. Yet, because God had David anointed by Samuel to be the next king of Israel, Saul's efforts to kill David (per Satan's ultimate plan to extinguish the lineage of Jesus), proved fruitless. Saul and his son Jonathan were both killed in battle, and David was made King of Israel.

David loved his son Absalom, yet Absalom proved to be an ally of Satan who plotted to steal David's kingdom: "But Absalom sent spies throughout all the tribes of Israel, saying, As soon as ye hear the sound of the trumpet, then ye shall say, Absalom reigneth in Hebron" (2 Samuel 15:10). Caught unawares with no standing army to defend the city, David was forced to retreat from Jerusalem when Absalom made his move. It wasn't until after Absalom was killed, that David returned to Jerusalem.

Solomon discovered that his elder brother Adonijah was an ally of Satan who "exalted himself, saying, I will be king" (1 Kings 1:5)—despite King David's stated decree that Solomon succeed him on the throne instead. Solomon was then made king, and Adonijah was humiliated at his pre-coronation party. Despite Adonijah's attempted usurpation, "Solomon said, If he will shew himself a worthy man, there shall not an hair of him fall to the earth: but if wickedness shall be found in him, he shall die" (1 Kings 1:52). Notwithstanding Solomon's pardon, Adonijah still continued to plot for the throne. When he made another move toward obtaining it, Solomon had him executed.

Though Solomon became known for his great wisdom, he still fell prey to his own lusts for foreign women acting as agents of the enemy. Despite God's admonition, he loved many enemies of Israel—"together with the daughter of Pharaoh, women of the Moabites, Ammonites, Edomites, Zidonians, *and* Hittites; Of the nations *concerning* which the LORD said unto the children of Israel, Ye shall not go in to them, neither shall they come in unto you: *for* surely they will turn away your heart after their gods" (1 Kings 11:1-2). They seduced Solomon into worshipping false gods. For having allowed his allegiance to be driven away from the one true God, he forfeited the united kingdom of Israel. While his family retained the tribes of Judah and Benjamin, the other ten tribes broke off and formed their own kingdom.

Identify Satan's Allies

Satan's allies come in many disguises. We see here an example of an old prophet acting as the devil's advocate in getting a young prophet to disobey God under the plausible pretense of holiness. The young prophet was sent to destroy an altar set up in Bethel on which offerings were made to calves of gold. After the altar was destroyed, the young prophet was commanded not to eat any bread or drink any water at that place, but leave town by a different way other than the way he came, and not turn back. While he rested under a tree outside of Bethel, the old prophet learned of his presence and approached him. "He said unto him, I *am* a prophet also as thou *art*; and an angel spake unto me by the word of the LORD, saying, Bring him back with thee into thine house, that he may eat bread and drink water. *But he lied unto him*" (1 Kings 13:18). Sadly for the young prophet, instead of praying for confirmation, he believed the man and followed him back to his home where he ate and drank with him in defiance of God's orders. For his gullibility in complying with the deception, "... when he was gone, a lion met him by the way, and slew him" (1 Kings 13:24). The young prophet should have awaited personal instruction from God, rather than relying on the hearsay of others. Direct marching orders cannot be rescinded except by superior officers. Yet no angel came to update the young prophet's situation. Believing in the unverified false report of an enemy agent cost him his life.

After the Babylonian captivity was ended through the conquest by Cyrus, he decreed that the Israelites may return to Jerusalem and rebuild their temple. Immediately, Satan employed allies to impede the work. "Then the people of the land weakened the hands of the people of Judah, and troubled them in building, And hired counsellors against them, to frustrate their purpose, all the days of Cyrus king of Persia, even until the reign of Darius king of Persia" (Ezra 4:4-5). Though hindered, the work slowly continued nevertheless until the reign of Artaxerxes, when two prominent allies of Satan, "Rehum the chancellor and Shimshai the scribe wrote a letter against Jerusalem to Artaxerxes" (Ezra 4:8) portraying the Jews as rebellious and contemptuous of the king. Artaxerxes then decreed that the rebuilding in Jerusalem cease. It wasn't until the later reign of Darius that an appeal was made to him referencing the previous Cyrus Decree—a decree that could not be rescinded—that the holy work was then allowed to continue under Darius' new affirming decree that the work not only be finished unhindered, but that it was also to be financed by Darius himself.

The reconstruction work continued under Nehemiah by decree of the king. "But it came to pass, *that* when Sanballat, and Tobiah, and the Arabians, and the Ammonites, and the Ashdodites, heard that the walls of Jerusalem were made up, *and* that the breaches began to be stopped, then they were very wroth, And conspired all of them together to come *and* to fight against Jerusalem, and to hinder it" (Nehemiah 4:7-8). We see how vigilant the enemy is in thwarting the people of God in their worship of Him. After Nehemiah's fervent prayers for protection and strength, however, the work continued. "And it came to pass, when our enemies heard that it was known unto us, and God had brought their counsel to nought, that we returned all of us to the wall, every one unto his work," (Nehemiah 4:15). Once Satan's allies are exposed and their plans revealed, then it is incumbent upon us to pray for protection against their devices, and for deliverance from their intended evil.

In the biblical book of Esther, we see just how bold Satan's allies can be. Not content with the thought of one man's destruction, Haman—one of Hitler's predecessors—plotted to have *all* Jews exterminated. After Mordecai the Jew refused to make obeisance to Haman the vile Agagite as he walked by, Haman was informed by his guards of the observed insult. He inquired as to who Mordecai was, and then into the background of his people. "And he thought scorn to lay hands on Mordecai alone; for they had shewed him the people of Mordecai: wherefore Haman sought to destroy all the Jews that *were* throughout the whole kingdom of Ahasuerus, *even* the people of Mordecai" (Esther 3:6). Haman, occupying a political position above all the princes in the kingdom, told the king in confidence a lie—that the Jews were a rebellious people determined to undermine the king's rule. The king then allowed Haman to decree the Jews as enemies to the kingdom, and named a day for their destruction—commanding the people of the realm to rise up and destroy the

Identify Satan's Allies

Jews on that day. It was also a decree that could not be rescinded. God, however, decreed a complete reversal of outcome. Haman was instead forced to honor Mordecai; his deceptive plot was revealed; he and his ten sons were hanged on the gallows he had built for Mordecai; and a new decree was issued for the Jews to fight and destroy those who were commanded to rise up against them—resulting in the deaths of over seventy-five thousand Jewish enemies.

In the book of Job, we see an example of how friends can be unwittingly turned into Satan's allies. Job was a righteous man, upright in the sight of God. Satan requested of God to have Job put to the test, claiming that it was easy for him to be righteous when he enjoyed such a good life of godly benefits, but take all that away, and Job would soon come to curse God. So God allowed the test. Satan afflicted Job first by having his sons and daughters die from a calamity, while his property was stolen by raiding Sabeans and Chaldeans. Despite those grievous losses, Job still blessed the Lord. Satan then afflicted Job's health with sore boils all over his body from head to toe. "Now when Job's three friends heard of all this evil that was come upon him, they came every one from his own place; Eliphaz the Temanite, and Bildad the Shuhite, and Zophar the Naamathite: for they had made an appointment together to come to mourn with him and to comfort him" (Job 2:7). Unhappily for Job, his friends were soon turned away from him by Satan. After seeing his pitiful condition, they became filled with a self-righteous spirit of judgment and assumed that Job's afflictions were well deserved because of some secret, unrepented sin on Job's part—for God punishes the wicked. Ignorant of God's design in allowing Satan to torment righteous Job unjustly so that Job could still praise Him and confound Satan, his friends became just another irritating boil adding to Job's misery. Their constant admonishments finally beat down poor Job until his faith wavered and he demanded an accounting from God as to what he had done to deserve this punishment. Note that the afflictions alone were not enough to break Job's faith. It wasn't until Satan employed agents—people very close to Job—that Satan was able to complete his mission. At this point, the Lord intervened and first chastised Job for daring to question Him. "Where wast thou when I laid the foundations of the earth? declare, if thou hast understanding" (Job 38:4). Job immediately humbled himself before God and repented of his foolishness. God then chastised more severely Job's friends for their part in causing Job to despair, when they should have supported him instead. For Job's stalwart defense of God throughout the ordeal (excepting that one wavering of faith), "the Lord gave Job twice as much as he had before" (Job 42:10). This example shows just how subtle Satan can be in using even our best friends to beat us down.

The biblical book of Isaiah provides us with a further example of Satan using various agents to undermine Israel as a whole and drive them from God. It is said that one bad apple can spoil the whole bunch. This is true because, as the apple decays, it emits noxious gases that are absorbed by surrounding apples which, in turn, affect those surrounding them until the entire barrel eventually becomes corrupted. One noxious attitude of apathy towards God can pervade an entire community if left undetected. Because of this domino effect, Israel had fallen away from God and righteousness; "Ah sinful nation, a people laden with iniquity, a seed of evildoers, children that are corrupters: they have forsaken the Lord, they have provoked the Holy One of Israel unto anger, they are gone away backward" (Isaiah 1:4). Their offerings of feigned repentance became meaningless physical acts devoid of any spiritual benefit to placate an angry God. "How is the faithful city become an harlot! it was full of judgment; righteousness lodged in it; but now murderers" (Isaiah 1:21). Satan's allies had promoted idolatry within Israel so that "they worship the work of their own hands, that which their own fingers have made" (Isaiah 2:8), instead of worshiping the one true God who made them all. Having violated the terms of their covenant with the Lord, they forfeited the protection of their one true ally. Assyria then successfully invaded and dispersed the Kingdom of Israel, resulting in the Ten Lost Tribes of Israel. The subsequent Babylonian invasions resulted in the captivity of the Kingdom of Judah in punishment as well for their treasonous idolatries against God.

Jeremiah was also a prophet sent to warn Israel of their sins to avoid the wrath of God. As he preached the message of repentance, he was often set upon by Satan's allies who rejected spiritual reformation and re-devotion to God. First, the men of Anathoth sought to kill Jeremiah, but the Lord thwarted their effort. Then, in their pride and arrogance, the priests, scribes, and elders who were deceived into believing that all was well with the Lord utterly rejected Jeremiah's warnings as having come from God. "Then said they, Come, and let us devise devices against Jeremiah; for the law shall not perish from the priest, nor counsel from the wise, nor the word from the prophet. Come, and let us smite him with the tongue, and let us not give heed to any of his words" (Jeremiah 18:18). Evil will always try to silence good.

Furthermore, "Then Pashur smote Jeremiah the prophet, and put him in the stocks that *were* in the high gate of Benjamin, which *was* by the house of the LORD" (Jeremiah 20:2). Jeremiah prophesied to Pashur that he and all his family would be taken captive to Babylon and die there, which they did. The Lord warned against the other prophets of Israel who had become compromised by Satan as well during this time of dire spiritual emergency; "Thus saith the LORD of hosts, Hearken not unto the words of the prophets that prophesy unto you: they make you vain: they speak a vision of their own heart, *and* not out of the mouth of the LORD" (Jeremiah 23:16). Not content with merely silencing Jeremiah (who would not be silenced), "Then spake the priests and the prophets unto the princes and to all the people, saying, This man *is* worthy to die; for he hath prophesied against this city, as ye have heard with your ears" (Jeremiah 26:11). God protected His messenger once again and delivered him from execution.

It wasn't long before another false prophet allied with Satan rose to counter the warnings of God spoken through Jeremiah. Hananiah delivered a false prophecy that, though Nebuchadnezzar of Babylon would indeed attack Jerusalem again, the Lord would break the yoke of Babylon and deliver Judah. Jeremiah responded: "The LORD hath not sent thee; but thou makest this people to trust in a lie. Therefore thus saith the LORD; Behold, I will cast thee from off the face of the earth: this year thou shalt die, because thou hast taught rebellion against the LORD" (Jeremiah 28:15-16). Two months later, Hananiah was dead. Despite all the false messages of deliverance and the false sense of security Satan's allies tried to instill in Judah, Jerusalem fell nonetheless and the people were taken into captivity in Babylon for the next seventy years as a divine punishment for their idolatries and apostasies.

We see in the book of Daniel several examples of how jealousy can create allies in Satan's cause. After the king had "made Daniel a great man, and gave him many great gifts, and made him ruler over the whole province of Babylon, and chief of the governors over all the wise *men* of Babylon .... Then Daniel requested of the king, and he set Shadrach, Meshach, and Abednego, over the affairs of the province of Babylon: but Daniel *sat* in the gate of the king" (Daniel 2:48-9). When the three Hebrew teenagers were elevated to positions of authority over the Babylonian people, there was great jealousy and indignation amongst certain Chaldeans in power. They became Satan's allies and plotted against those holy children of God. They told the king "There are certain Jews whom thou hast set over the affairs of the province of Babylon, Shadrach, Meshach, and Abednego; these men, O king, have not regarded thee: they serve not thy gods, nor worship the golden image which thou hast set up" (Daniel 3:12). When the king confronted them, they confirmed that they could not worship a golden image of Nebuchadnezzar, despite the royal decree to do so. He had them thrown into a fiery furnace. But the Lord was with them. They emerged from the furnace unharmed, and without even the slightest whiff of smoke upon them.

Another example in the biblical book of Daniel shows Satan gathering allies to destroy that renowned man of God. It occurred when "... Daniel was preferred above the presidents and princes, because an excellent spirit *was* in him; and the king thought to set him over the whole realm. Then the presidents and princes sought to find occasion against Daniel concerning the kingdom" (Daniel 6:3-4). Because Daniel was an upright man of God, no civil corruption or fault could be found within him. His enemies, Satan's allies, knew that they would have to attack Daniel somehow through his religious zeal and turn a positive attribute into a negative liability. They devised a plan. "All the presidents of the kingdom, the governors, and the princes, the counsellors, and the captains, have consulted together to establish a royal statute, and to make a firm decree, that whosoever shall ask a petition of any God or man for thirty days, save of thee, O king, he shall be cast into the den of lions" (Daniel 6:7). They knew that Daniel was a devout, praying man, who gave thanks to God in prayer three times daily and, therefore, would never obey the new law to forsake God in favor of the king. As expected, Daniel continued his reverential practice boldly, even praying in front of open windows in his home. The plotters then appeared on schedule to catch Daniel praying in violation of the king's decree, which could not be rescinded. For that, he was thrown into the lions' den. Yet Daniel's reliable ally—the God of Israel—was greater than the combined multitude of Satan's allies. Under God's command, the lions did Daniel no harm during the night. When the king saw this the next morning, he was glad in his heart for he admired and respected Daniel. The king then realized the wicked plot of those men who had accused Daniel. He had them, with their wives and children, thrown into the same den of punishment, where their bodies were immediately torn to pieces by the lions.

As we've seen above, in just the few examples cited of many more, the Old Testament is rife with episodes of betrayal and treachery inspired by agents of the devil. We see further examples exposing Satan's allies in the New Testament as well. The most obvious examples are the actions of Judas Iscariot acting as a double agent for the enemy in the apostle/betrayer role; the Jewish elders acting as prosecutors of the Messiah; and the peoples' actions of complicity in condemning the Lord before Pontius Pilate.

At Jesus' birth, Satan compelled others to do his will to destroy the newly incarnated King of kings. He gained an ally in King Herod by inspiring the fear of the prophesized king now being born, to end his reign. Herod tried to trick visiting wise men that had come to see the new King to reveal His location to him after they had found Him, but they saw through his evil design and departed the country another way. "Then Herod, when he saw that he was mocked of the wise men, was exceeding wroth, and sent forth, and slew all the children that were in Bethlehem, and in all the coasts thereof, from two years old and under, according to the time which he had diligently inquired of the wise men" (Matthew 2:16). Joseph and Mary, allied with God, were led safely beforehand into Egypt to escape the slaughter.

We see Jesus' fellow citizens of Nazareth upbraiding and rejecting Him: "And they were offended in him. But Jesus said unto them, A prophet is not without honour, save in his own country, and in his own house" (Matthew 13:57). Through their familiarity with Jesus, "Is not this the carpenter's son?" (Matthew 13:55), Satan was able to breed contempt in Jesus' own hometown through the indignant thoughts that this local boy couldn't possibly be the long-awaited Messiah. Satan incited hatred in their hearts so that they "...thrust him out of the city, and led him unto the brow of the hill whereon their city was built, that they might cast him down headlong" (Luke 4:29). But Jesus simply walked through the crowd of hateful conspirators and departed.

Though Jesus went about teaching repentance and a return unto holy God, His fellow Rabbis became allied with God's great enemy against Him. "Then went the Pharisees, and took counsel how they might entangle him in *his* talk" (Matthew 22:15). As they sought to trip Him up over taxation, Jesus' wisdom confounded them all; "Then saith he unto them, Render therefore unto Caesar the things which are Caesar's; and unto God the things that are God's" (Matthew 22:21). They could do nothing further over this foiled trap, and departed.

In what is probably the greatest act of betrayal in human history, we see an ally of Satan feigning an act of love to perpetrate his treason. When the chief priests and elders sought to have Jesus arrested, they needed someone to identify Him for the guards. "Now he that betrayed him gave them a sign, saying, Whomsoever I shall kiss, that same is he: hold him fast. And forthwith he came to Jesus, and said, Hail, master; and kissed him" (Matthew 26:48-9). Jesus responded: "Judas, betrayest thou the Son of man with a kiss?" (Luke 22:48). In this episode, we see definitively how those closest to us may still be turned against us.

In times of stress and duress, no one can be trusted except

Identify Satan's Allies

Jesus, who will never leave or forsake us. After Jesus' arrest, when He should have been comforted by the support of His disciples, Peter denied three separate times that he even knew Jesus. Jesus' own allies were turned against Him. The people, who had benefited greatly from the myriad of Jesus' miracles of healing, along with His exposition of deep scriptural mysteries, nevertheless turned against Him at His trial. When Pilate honored the Jewish tradition of releasing one prisoner on the Passover feast, he asked the crowd if he should release Jesus or the murderer Barabbas. Despite all the recent good that Jesus had done for them, they chose Barabbas over Jesus. "And the governor said, Why, what evil hath he done? But they cried out the more, saying, Let him be crucified" (Matthew 27:23). Jesus was then handed over to Satan's other steadfast allies, the Roman soldiers, who mocked, spat upon Him, and beat Him, before nailing Him to a cross to die a most horrible death.

Despite having lived with Jesus for years, and having heard His constant message of love and forgiveness firsthand, some of His own apostles were subverted by Satan. The Samaritans had rejected Jesus because He was determined to go to Jerusalem to worship, instead of to their temple on Mount Gerizim; "And when his disciples James and John saw *this*, they said, Lord, wilt thou that we command fire to come down from heaven, and consume them, even as Elias did?" (Luke 9:54). Those apostles were willing to destroy the Samaritans because of a national prejudice fostered by Satan, for which Jesus naturally rebuked them.

We see a further example of Satan seeking allies by sowing pride and division amongst the apostles: "And there was also a strife among them, which of them should be accounted the greatest" (Luke 22:24). Jesus taught humility by example. He came down from His glorious throne in heaven to live as a humble carpenter and to suffer the abuses of His enemies. Yet the apostles were deceived into magnifying themselves. Jesus corrected them by teaching instead that the *least* shall be considered the greatest—that the *humble* shall be exalted, and the proud will be abased.

After Jesus' crucifixion and resurrection, we see a perfect example of Satan employing his agents to undermine the integrity of the fledgling church. Ananias and his wife Sapphira were, on the surface, disciples of Christ. Yet underneath, they were filled with a spirit of ambition, and merely sought positions of authority in the new church hierarchy as eminent disciples. Their hearts were filled with pride and deception instead of humility and an eagerness to serve. Their deception began when they sold a piece of land. To facilitate their advancement by appearing magnanimous, they boldly lied in saying that they had turned over the entire proceeds to the church, when, in fact, they had withheld a portion of the money for themselves. In attempting to lie to the Holy Spirit of truth and infiltrate the church as enemy agents from the start, they condemned themselves. Ananias fell dead before the gathered assembly as soon as he spoke the lie. Sapphira returned later seeking her husband, and, when confronted, repeated the lie and also fell dead on the spot.

When Stephen began preaching the gospel of Christ, Satan immediately found allies to silence him. "Then there arose certain of the synagogue, which is called *the synagogue* of the Libertines, and Cyrenians, and Alexandrians, and of them of Cilicia and of Asia, disputing with Stephen" (Acts 6:9). The Christian message of repentance and forgiveness—which breaks Satan's chains that bind us in sin and condemnation—could not be allowed to be disseminated. The agents of the devil were incensed. "Then they cried out with a loud voice, and stopped their ears, and ran upon him with one accord, And cast *him* out of the city, and stoned *him*: and the witnesses laid down their clothes at a young man's feet, whose name was Saul" (Acts 7:57–8). Saul of Tarsus was Satan's greatest ally at the time who "... made havock of the church, entering into every house, and haling men and women committed *them* to prison" (Acts 8:3). Deceived into thinking that he was doing the will of God, he relentlessly persecuted the first Christians.

We will now see that though Satan can turn some people into acting as his enemy agents against the godly, that avenue of attack has become a two-way street thanks to repentance and forgiveness under Christ crucified and resurrected. Though a rarer occurrence, Satan's allies can be turned away from being agents of evil into agents of God to fight against sin. Saul of Tarsus is one such example. He became the chief persecutor of Christians shortly after the Sanhedrin had Jesus put to death. In his zealotry towards God, he admitted retrospectively: "I persecuted this way unto the death, binding and delivering into prisons both men and women. As also the high priest doth bear me witness, and all the estate of the elders: from whom also I received letters unto the brethren, and went to Damascus, to bring them which were there bound unto Jerusalem, for to be punished" (Acts 22:4-5). Beforehand, however, while on his way to Damascus, Jesus spoke to him from heaven and revealed that He was the Messiah, and that Saul had been unjustly persecuting Jesus' believers. Saul was immediately transformed into one of history's greatest evangelists for Christ—the apostle Paul.

Many further examples occurred of Christ turning enemies into allies after His Holy Spirit descended upon the earth on Pentecost. On one particular day, three thousand souls were converted to Christ. Two thousand more were converted at another time after hearing Peter and John speak. Cornelius the Roman centurion and his family became Christians after hearing Peter preach. These events began the wholesale conversion around the globe of Gentile unbelievers into Christian warriors, striking a great blow to Satan's power on earth.

Yet, Satan will never cease to recruit allies to silence the message of Christ. He employed King Herod to have the apostle James executed. Herod also had Peter arrested, and planned to execute him as well—until an angel of God acted on Peter's behalf and facilitated his escape from prison. Satan engaged allies to hinder Paul's missionary journey in many ways—as Paul recounts in 2 Corinthians 11:25: "Thrice was I beaten with rods, once was I stoned, thrice I suffered shipwreck, a night and a day I have been in the deep." Satan even sowed discord in the disciples over certain practices such as circumcision and eating rituals. When Paul and Barnabas were preaching on the Isle of Paphos, Elymas the sorcerer "withstood them, seeking to turn away the deputy from the faith" (Acts 13:8). He failed in his efforts "because greater is he that is in you, than he that is in the world" (1 John 4:4). The power of our alliance with Christ through the Holy Spirit overpowers the allies of the enemy.

Satan will remain active in recruiting allies to his cause until he is finally vanquished by the armies of Christ at His second coming. We see that activity constantly exposed in our own daily lives. We've all read about multiple lawsuits filed against organized religion over the past few decades for ignoring the existence of pedophiles within the clergy who abused children under their guidance, per Satan's promptings. Political movements today allied with Satan actively promote every biblical sin God has decreed an abomination. Corrupted judicial activists on the bench protect Satan's allies from prosecution— even pardoning convicted pre-meditated killers of police. Devout Christians everywhere are targeted and persecuted for their beliefs by the secular allies of the devil as being intolerant and hateful when, in fact, delivering the Christian message of salvation from the bondage in sin is an act of the greatest love. For many, Satan has effectively turned the world upside down so that evil is called good, and good is called evil.

We can learn from these many examples how vigilant we must remain, and how focused on Scripture we need to be to protect us from the poison of secret enemies. We've seen in the examples listed above how Satan can divide husbands and wives like Adam and Eve; how Israel's men were led astray by intermarrying with foreign women; how brothers like Cain and Abel, Moses and Aaron, and Joseph's and Solomon's siblings can be turned against them. We've seen how the children of Eli and the children of King David were corrupted against their fathers' godliness. Job's best friends became his greatest tormenters under Satan's guile. The tribe of Benjamin revolted against greater Israel for defending one of Satan's agents. David's own king, whom he served faithfully and valiantly, became an enemy agent working against Israel by constantly seeking David's destruction. Prophets of God have been compromised into lying and deceiving fellow prophets. Religious leaders have been instrumental in punishing and persecuting prophets such as Jeremiah, who were sent to deliver God's message of repentance and reformation in Israel. Even James and John, apostles of Christ, were subverted into entertaining delusions of grandeur over their fellow apostles. Identifying Satan's allies, in whatever form they may assume, is imperative in order to retain our religious integrity and unwavering faith, and to win the spiritual battle for our souls.

11

Know the Final Outcome

While watching an adventure movie or reading a spy novel, it is easy to become anxious over the outcome. As we see a common formula play out—of the heroes being thwarted and hope being extinguished—we wonder if evil has actually won, or if good can finally prevail . . . somehow. These are the questions which trouble the viewer/reader until the end of the movie/book, when the full outcome is revealed. Until then, the circumstantial evidence of the times indicates a losing battle, depriving us of hope in victory. In real life, these ominous signs can instill an inclination towards surrender.

Fortunately for us, as Christian warriors, we already know the final conclusion of our spiritual war and do not have to suffer that stress. We've seen the end of the movie. We've read the end of the book. Sun Tzu acknowledged "Thus, what enables ... the good general to ... conquer, and achieve things beyond the reach of ordinary men, is *foreknowledge*" (*ch*.XIII, *ss*.4). We know that Christ is victorious, and that Satan is utterly defeated. With that foreknowledge, we can take solace in victory during the individual spiritual battles in our lives, and become emboldened to fight courageously and steadfastly to the end during Satan's collective war against humanity. It is imperative, therefore, to be on the winning side, as the results of victory are eternal and irreversible.

During the early years of WWII, the British suffered many military defeats against the German army—from Dunkirk, to Singapore, to North Africa. When German Field Marshall Rommel was finally turned back by British forces at El Alamein, British Prime Minister Winston Churchill (1874-1965) stated "... we have a new experience. We have a victory—a remarkable and

Know the Final Outcome

definite victory." The British were given a renewed spirit of hope. Without becoming overconfident, though, Churchill then cautioned, "Now this is not the end. It is not even the beginning of the end. But it is, perhaps, the end of the beginning." Humility in victory is needed to maintain momentum and avoid the pitfalls of overconfidence.

Yet another more remarkable victory, which gives us even greater hope, occurred thousands of years prior, when Jesus Christ was born, crucified, and resurrected. When God became incarnate in this world as the long-awaited Messiah in the body of the baby Jesus, the spiritual endgame had begun. The "beginning" occurred in the Garden of Eden after the fall of humanity into sin, when God first promised a Redeemer: "And I will put enmity between thee and the woman, and between thy seed and her seed; it shall bruise thy head, and thou shalt bruise his heel" (Genesis 3:15). The "end of the beginning" occurred on the cross, when Jesus was crucified. Before the crucifixion, Satan had full-spectrum dominance over occupied earth. Demonic possession was quite prevalent in the world. We know this because we read of many instances in the Gospels of Jesus exorcising demons from various individuals. It appeared initially to the apostles that after Jesus was crucified, all hope was lost. However, when Jesus conquered death, hell, and the grave through His resurrection, hope was restored. The power of Satan on earth was greatly diminished (demonic possession is much rarer today than it was then)—reducing and limiting Satan's artillery, for the most part, to bluff and deceit. It was the fulfillment of Scripture, marking "the beginning of the end" of Satan's kingdom.

As in most mystery books, Holy Scripture also contains many clues as to the final aftermath of the battle between good and evil. Many of these clues are couched in prophecy. "Behold, the former things are come to pass, and new things do I declare: before they spring forth I tell you of them" (Isaiah 42:9). In the book of Daniel, we are provided with a great spoiler prophecy, regarding the end-times: "And at that time shall Michael stand up, the great prince which standeth for the children of thy people: and there shall be a time of trouble, such as never was since there was a nation *even* to that same time: and at that time thy people shall be delivered, every one that shall be found written in the book" (Daniel 12:1). This comforts us that every believer in Christ will be delivered from the Great Tribulation to come, when judgment is passed upon the unbelieving world.

Many other such prophecies in Scripture contribute to paint a fuller picture of the victory ahead so that any studious reader of the Bible gains the advantage of knowing the conclusion over the secular multitudes, who are "... without understanding; which have eyes, and see not; which have ears, and hear not" (Jeremiah 5:21). Here are a few select disclosing passages:

- "The LORD shall cause thine enemies that rise up against thee to be smitten before thy face: they shall come out against thee one way, and flee before thee seven ways" (Deuteronomy 28:7).
- "Thou shalt break them with a rod of iron; thou shalt dash them in pieces like a potter's vessel" (Psalm 2:9).
- "The LORD said unto my Lord, Sit thou at my right hand, until I make thine enemies thy footstool" (Psalm 110:1).
- "[H]e shall smite the earth with the rod of his mouth, and with the breath of his lips shall he slay the wicked" (Isaiah 11:4).
- "O Jerusalem, the holy city: for henceforth there shall no more come into thee the uncircumcised and the unclean" (Isaiah 52:1).
- "Behold, the days come, saith the LORD, that I will raise unto David a righteous Branch, and a King shall reign and prosper, and shall execute judgment and justice in the earth" (Jeremiah 23:5).
- "And I will make them one nation in the land upon the mountains of Israel; and one king shall be king to them all" (Ezekiel 37:22).
- "For the vision *is* yet for an appointed time, but at the end it shall speak, and not lie: though it tarry, wait for it; because it will surely come, it will not tarry" (Habakkuk 2:3).

- "Then shall he say also unto them on the left hand, Depart from me, ye cursed, into everlasting fire, prepared for the devil and his angels" (Matthew 25:41).
- "[Jesus] shall be great, and shall be called the Son of the Highest: and the Lord God shall give unto him the throne of his father David: And he shall reign over the house of Jacob for ever; and of his kingdom there shall be no end" (Luke 1:32-3).
- "These things I have spoken unto you, that in me ye might have peace. In the world ye shall have tribulation: but be of good cheer; I have overcome the world" (John 16:33).
- "Therefore being a prophet, and knowing that God had sworn with an oath to him, that of the fruit of his loins, according to the flesh, he would raise up Christ to sit on his throne" (Acts 2:30).
- "Then *cometh* the end, when he shall have delivered up the kingdom to God, even the Father; when he shall have put down all rule and all authority and power. For he must reign, till he hath put all enemies under his feet" (1 Corinthians 15:24-5).
- "[T]he Lord Jesus shall be revealed from heaven with his mighty angels, In flaming fire taking vengeance on them that know not God, and that obey not the gospel of our Lord Jesus Christ: Who shall be punished with everlasting destruction from the presence of the Lord, and from the glory of his power" (2 Thessalonians 1:7-9).
- "... God spared not the angels that sinned, but cast *them* down to hell, and delivered *them* into chains of darkness, to be reserved unto judgment" (2 Peter 2:4).
- "He that committeth sin is of the devil; for the devil sinneth from the beginning. For this purpose the Son of God was manifested, that he might destroy the works of the devil" (1 John 3:8).

Those prophetic verses absolutely reveal that the devil loses, and Jesus wins. The temporary prince of this world will be overthrown by the everlasting Prince of Peace, who will establish His kingdom on a renewed earth, forever.

The Revelation of John provides many definitive details regarding the final struggle between Christ's army and Satan's army;

> And the beast was taken, and with him the false prophet that wrought miracles before him, with which he deceived them that had received the mark of the beast, and them that worshipped his image. These both were cast alive into a lake of fire burning with brimstone. And the remnant were slain with the sword of him that sat upon the horse, which *sword* proceeded out of his mouth: and all the fowls were filled with their flesh.
> (Revelation 19:20-21)

Having Satan's Supreme Commander, the Antichrist, along with his chief propagandist the False Prophet disposed of, the Commander-in-Chief of the axis of evil will then be dealt with accordingly: "And the devil that deceived them was cast into the lake of fire and brimstone, where the beast and the false prophet *are*, and shall be tormented day and night for ever and ever" (Revelation 20:10). The final reveal is unambiguous.

We must access all of that provided foreseen postwar intel from the Scriptures in order to maintain hope in our lives and to fortify us spiritually during this long war. The apostle John was shown a vision of the total victory, which he reports to us: "And I saw a new heaven and a new earth: for the first heaven and the first earth were passed away; and there was no more sea" (Revelation 21:1). Therefore, we must look forward with joyful anticipation to that day of triumphant victory and never become dismayed in the interim.

Part 2: Society

12

Love and Marriage

In wartime, while it is necessary to employ proper weapons and armor on the field of battle during open warfare, it is also necessary to employ proper intelligence behind the lines to discover and thwart the enemy's tactics, as well as to neutralize his subtle propaganda campaign to recruit allies and undermine national resolve. Prussian King Frederick the Great (1712–1786) observed that "The art of war is divided between force and stratagem. What cannot be done by force must be done by stratagem." That's why in addition to a Department of Defense, all nations also have some sort of Intelligence Agency.

It was noted in the Introduction to this work that most interrelational ailments have root causes which have been sown and watered by Satan through his corrosive propaganda campaign. Because of the heavy assault on religion and morality, over the past few decades especially, scriptural radar—once used to detect truth—has been all but confounded by the enemy's deceitful, misinforming, and indoctrinating chaff being regularly dispersed during these so-called "progressive" times. Spiritual fact eludes discovery so that secular falsehood finds receptive hosts across the full spectrum of society and culture. It is only through scriptural knowledge that can we analyze the data in order to discover actionable intelligence, and then fortify our spiritual position against that uncovered deceit through intervention. Satan understands that when he weakens us spiritually as individuals, he weakens the nation collectively; that a nation under God forfeits its divine protection when it becomes a nation absent God. That is his ultimate outward goal—to undermine faith within by sowing seeds of doubt, division, despair, and defeat in all aspects of our lives. It is this incremental erosion of faith that defines his guerilla warfare tactics. Literally taken, *guerilla* means *little war*. Our souls are under daily onslaught by his hit-and-run skirmishes designed to grind down our spiritual fortifications.

After Adam's creation, "... the Lord God said, It is not good that the man should be alone; I will make him an help meet for him" (Genesis 2:18). He then created the woman, Eve, so that the two of them could be fruitful and multiply the human race. The institution of marriage—established by God from the beginning of humanity for all earthly time—is between a man and a woman; "Therefore shall a man ... cleave unto his wife: and they shall be one flesh" (Genesis 2:24). Two bonded together are stronger than one standing alone. Marriage is the foundation of the family, and the nuclear family is the cornerstone of civilization. It predates government, for without marriage and children, there is no society. Without society, there is no need for governmental rules and regulations. It is only natural, then, that Satan would start by compromising the substructure of marriage in his attempt to undermine the fortifications of humanity, and attempt to pull down all that God has commanded us to build up.

The benefits of marriage are legion. Men and women who are married are happier and healthier than those who are single. Depression is lower in married people with families because they provide needed emotional support to the partner in distress. On average, married couples accumulate more wealth and enjoy greater prosperity over those who are single. Married women are at lower risk for domestic violence and violent crime than single women. Marriage protects children against poverty, insecurity, and emotional illnesses such as depression and thoughts of suicide. New studies prove that children of divorced parents do worse in school than do children of continuously married parents. Boys raised without both parents are at much greater risk of engaging in criminal behavior. The youth of any nation determines its future. "A good tree cannot bring forth evil fruit, neither *can* a corrupt tree bring forth good fruit" (Matthew 7:18). By corrupting the tree of marriage, Satan ensures a greater harvest of corruption in our youth. Noted American philosopher Will Durant (1885–1981) sensibly described the importance of the family:

The family has been the ultimate foundation of every civilization known to history. It was the economic and productive unit of society, tilling the land together; it was the political unit of society, with parental authority as the supporting microcosm of the State. It was the cultural unit, transmitting letters and arts, rearing and teaching the young; and it was the moral unit, inculcating through cooperative work and discipline, those social dispositions which are the psychological basis and cement of civilized society. In many ways it was more essential than the state: governments might break up and order yet survive, if the family remained; whereas it seemed to sociologists that if the family should dissolve, civilization itself would disappear.[43]

The attempts to destroy marriage are many. Satan is the ultimate totalitarian—working towards setting up a one-world dictatorial government under his powerful general, Antichrist. As such, he requires *total* devotion. He will suffer no split allegiances. The Revelation of John tells us that those who refuse to take his mark will be beheaded. Therefore, it is not unusual that those under his persuasion have also utilized methods to achieve totalitarian goals as well by starting with the destruction of the family. We've seen it historically under fascists, communists, and socialists. Hitler infamously recruited the German youth in his Nazi movement and had them swear fealty to him even over their own families. History sadly witnessed many German youths turning in their parents to the Gestapo to be tortured and executed for speaking out against Hitler's evil. In the *Communist Manifesto,* German political theorist Karl Marx (1818–1883) called for the "abolition of the family." Today, Big Government Socialism (aka Big-Daddy Government) replaces the family in many countries.

After Marx' death, fellow German philosopher and co-author of the *Communist Manifesto,* Friedrich Engels (1820–1895), noted "It is a peculiar fact that with every great revolutionary move-

---

43 Durant, W. J. (1920). *The Mansions of Philosophy.* Garden City, NY: Garden City Publ. doi:https://ia800400.us.archive.org/12/items/TheMansionsOfPhilosophy_201605/Binder2.pdf, pp. 395-6.

ment the question of 'free love' comes to the foreground."⁴⁴ The *free love* movement of the countercultural 1960s greatly helped to undermine the institution of marriage on a global basis. Today, there is a renewed effort by socialists and atheists to redefine the institution of marriage between one man and one woman into a relationship between whomever—two men; two women; adults and children; humans and animals. As a result of expanding the definition of marriage to meaninglessness, we've recently witnessed in China the perverse marriage of a man to his inanimate sex doll.

In a 5–4 split decision, five unelected justices of the U.S. Supreme Court bowed to a misnomered political "correctness" and overruled God in the civics arena by nullifying His five thousand-year-old definition of marriage as between one man and one woman. In the 2015 *Obergfell v Hodges* case, the court ruled that all fifty states must recognize and perform same-sex marriages. Those who fought to retain the former, traditional definition of heterosexual marriage were persecuted viciously and relentlessly by the advocates for same-sex marriage. Before the Supreme Court decision was finally issued, many lives and careers of people advocating for California's ballot proposition (Prop 8), to preserve the traditional view of marriage, were destroyed.

The courts have also facilitated the break-up of marriage through no-fault divorce, making it easier to breach the marital contract and abandon one's vows—by abandoning the requirement to show any wrongdoing by either party. Mainstream media outlets like *The New York Times* advocate for open, non-monogamous marriages, involving many partners.⁴⁵ The increasing prevalence of pornography in our culture contributes to the assault on marriage by fostering infidelity to the sexual union between husband and wife. As a result, we are now seeing record rates of divorce in the baby boomer generation—those born between the years of 1946–

---

44 Friedrich Engels, 'Das Buch der Offenbarung', in Marx-Engels Werke (Berlin, 1959; henceforth MEW), XXI, p. 10.

45 Dominus, Susan. "Is an Open Marriage a Happier Marriage?" The New York Times. May 11, 2017. Accessed May 21, 2018. https://www.nytimes.com/2017/05/11/magazine/is-an-open-marriage-a-happier-marriage.html.

1964.[46] With all these things actively working against the concept of monogamous fidelity, it is no surprise, then, that marriage rates in the United States are at their lowest levels recorded in a century.

Even before marriage occurs, Satan works actively to hinder fulfilling, stable relationships between men and women. While people are still single, he fosters a sense of loneliness in individuals by distancing them from our ever-present God with worldly distractions. Then he compounds that emotional isolation with anxiety and impatience so that individuals rush into companionship with incompatible candidates—only to be set up for eventual heartbreak as insurmountable character differences become highlighted in the relationship, and budding love is slowly extinguished. After the breakup, people become reluctant to enter into further relationships and end up doubling-down on emotional isolation—the original cause of their rush to companionship—to avoid further heartbreak. Falling out of love is listed in many polls as the top reason for the demise of relationships. Therefore, it is better to *pray and wait* for the right person to come along, than rush into failure. "Delight thyself also in the LORD; and he shall give thee the desires of thine heart" (Psalm 37:4). It is the Lord who brings true soul mates together.

Satan uses other means as well to sow seeds of discontent in personal relationships. He exploits financial stresses to drive wedges between people—especially those actively in love. Financial stress creates elements of tension such as insecurity, irritability, fear, depression, and bodily illness—all of which strain relationships. We can deny Satan the victory of division during financial woes by dwelling upon scriptural verses of comfort. Jesus "... said unto his disciples, Therefore I say unto you, Take no thought for your life, what ye shall eat; neither for the body, what ye shall put on. ... Consider the ravens: for they neither sow nor reap; which neither have storehouse nor barn; and God feedeth them: how much more are ye better than the fowls?" (Luke 12:22–24). It is also necessary to "... remember the LORD thy God: for *it is*

---

[46] Crowley, Jocelyn Elise. "Why Are so Many Baby Boomers Getting Divorced?" The Week - All You Need to Know about Everything That Matters. May 21, 2018. Accessed May 21, 2018. http://theweek.com/articles/772106/why-are-many-baby-boomers-getting-divorced.

he that giveth thee power to get wealth, that he may establish his covenant which he sware unto thy fathers, as *it is* this day" (Deuteronomy 8:18). God is the ultimate philanthropist in our lives. We are merely His instruments for the distribution and allocation of those resources. Trust in Him during financial hardships and He *will* carry us through them.

Another method of destroying relationships is through Satan's exploitation of the human weakness for immoral or illegal pleasure, also known as the forbidden-fruit syndrome. It worked in the Garden of Eden to sever Adam and Eve's fidelity to God through the sin of disobedience. It's been working ever since. Infidelity affects 25 percent of marital relationships. It fosters anger through betrayal, as well as guilt in both parties. It is an effective enticement Satan employs to undermine devotion. We can combat the temptation first by remembering and embracing the teaching of Jesus: "What therefore God hath joined together, let not man put asunder" (Matthew 19:6). Then, we need to remind ourselves of our solemn marital vows uttered before God and an assembly of family and friends *to have and to hold, from this day forward, for better, for worse, for richer, for poorer, in sickness and in health, until death do us part*. We need to reinforce those vows daily through words and deeds that indicate how much we love and care for our spouse. Those demonstrated acts of love will increase the desire on behalf of both parties to remain faithful to each other.

Fostering jealousy is another method Satan uses to divide and conquer happy couples. If unfounded, it creates unnecessary stress and drama, which erodes bonds of love. An unhealthy jealousy is a poisonous mix of insecurity, fear, and selfishness. It cultivates distrust through paranoia, which destroys relationships by instilling a sense of obsession and possession. Demanding an accounting of a partner's free time is dictatorial. Demanding 100 percent of a partner's free time—to the exclusion of his or her family and friends—is a domination and control issue which throws the relationship out of harmonic, egalitarian balance, while it simultaneously destroys self-esteem in the dominated partner. The root cause of a desire for control can be found in a quote from Milton's *Paradise Lost* about Satan's underlying attitude, that it is "Better to reign in hell than serve in heaven." The desire of one partner to *reign* over the other creates a hell on-earth for the other partner.

Jealousy, however, can be used constructively to animate conversation between couples who may have been neglecting each other, or who have allowed minimal flaws in their relationship to fester into maximum problems. By addressing concerns head-on, the marital relationship can be strengthened through a healthy jealousy. "Love is patient and kind; it is not jealous or conceited or proud" (1 Corinthians 13:4). It is sometimes necessary to rekindle the fire which has died down, and fan it back into active flames to save the relationship. Every fire needs a constant supply of fresh fuel or it burns out.

Boredom, therefore, becomes something else to be on our guard against. Satan uses familiarity to breed contempt. When the excitement of falling in love wanes, he tempts us with a longing to relive that excitement. Then, we are apt to forget that falling in love is only the *beginning* of a long-term relationship. That initial fire and fervor is used to forge a solid foundation for building a devoted love upon—over time. Though the flare-up of a newly ignited welding torch is very bright, it is the duller, sharpened blue-flame cone that accomplishes the actual welding. It is that devoted love which endures over the giddy crush of infatuation. The moderate campfire is easier to maintain than the raging bonfire.

Accordingly, we must learn to see that every new stage in our relationship comes with its own set of challenges and adventures. It is how we react to those challenges—with either boredom or excitement—that matters. For example, many young women are taught today that being a stay-at-home mom is a tedious waste of their lives. Yet, the excitement and challenge of raising children is experienced daily for those with eyes to see. The fulfillment of being parents who successfully raise good and productive children (through sacrificing their own time and resources) cannot be diminished by a society demanding that all individuals live for themselves instead and build a career to bring about self-satisfaction. Let's face it; most jobs consist of boring repetition. Most of everyday life—the daily grind—is boring routine. We will not wake up every day to a new and thrilling adventure, as many seem to expect in their youthful exuberance and naiveté. Those unrealistic expectations will quickly sink a person into dissatisfaction and boredom. Raising children, however, can be a new adventure every day as any stay-at-home parent will tell you. It is helpful to remember the words of St. Paul: "... for I have learned, in whatsoever state I am, *therewith* to be content" (Philippians 4:11). Contentment is the antidote to the poison of boredom. Its focus is inward toward what you have, rather than outward toward what you don't have.

Inequality in any relationship can be destructive as well. It denies one partner the freedom to rise up and be the person he or she truly is. It manifests in different ways. There is the inequality of power, in which one partner makes all of the decisions. Decisions should be allocated by agreement, such as one person handling the finances, while the other person handles the household maintenance, etc. But when one person takes it upon himself or herself to make *all* of the decisions in the relationship, there is a destructive, dictatorial inequality present. Absolute power corrupts absolutely, and abuses inevitably follow.

The refusal of one partner ever to compromise or apologize is also indicative of inequality in a relationship. It reveals in that person a certain narcissistic belief that he or she is never wrong. It is a dangerous and delusional self-importance which automatically relegates the partner to inferior status. Constant criticism of one partner by the other also reinforces that sense of inferiority, and lowers self-esteem in the criticized partner—thereby guaranteeing destruction of that relationship.

Inequality in finances can also fuel inequality in a relationship. Instead of pooling all household income for the greater good of the family (to fulfill the marital contract agreed upon by both parties), and then allowing for some discretionary recreational spending on top of the finances for the personal enjoyment of both, the spouse who earns more may choose to withhold a large portion of the money he or she has earned for personal use. Then, what generally follows is that the other partner, who earns less, is forced to spend his or her entire income on joint goods for the family, leaving no funds available for personal expenditures. Withholding income, by succumbing to a prideful and selfish entitlement attitude, works to the detriment of the family unit by creating resentment through unequal resource allocation. Rather than viewing all income and/or household labor from either partner as *equal input*, that spouse chooses to accept a division of worth—usually defined by the main breadwinner (working eight to twelve hours a day out of the home), with no input from the main laborer (working eighteen hours a day in the home). Keeping one's checkbook secret from the other partner is a good indicator that inequality for personal indulgence over the family common cause exists.

In Matthew 20:1-15, Jesus used a parable to explain how all work towards the common goal was equally valuable in the eyes of God. Workers were hired early in the morning for a day's wage. Several hours later, more workers were hired. This continued throughout the day, even up to the last hour. When it came time to pay the workers, they all received the *same* wage for they had all labored towards the common goal of working the vineyard. This caused grumbling among those who had labored longer in those equal efforts during the day. A prideful elevation of one's contribution over the other comes from Satan and needs to be identified immediately and rejected, before resentment can be allowed to develop. "And let us not be weary in well doing: for in due season we shall reap, if we faint not" (Galatians 6:9). When we wholly commit to marriage and raising a family—as the workers agreed to the terms of their pay—then we are not to compare input between partners for disparity of time, labor, and/or income.

Though there are many other root causes which can undermine relationships which we need to be on our guard against, probably the most perilous for a Christian is spiritual incompatibility—being married to an atheist. "Be ye not unequally yoked together with unbelievers: for what fellowship hath righteousness with unrighteousness? and what communion hath light with darkness? And what concord hath Christ with Belial? or what part hath he that believeth with an infidel?" (2 Corinthians 6:14-15). Though it has happened that unbelievers have been converted to faith through a partner's ministrations and prayers, it is a rare occurrence and should not be counted upon by the believer, for "The wind bloweth where it listeth, and thou hearest the sound thereof, but canst not tell whence it cometh, and whither it goeth: so is every one that is born of the Spirit" (John 3:8). We cannot control who will receive the Spirit and be converted. Such expectations almost always lead to disappointment initially, and then to dissolution of spiritual hope finally. Many relationships are doomed from the outset through the belief that one person can change the marriage partner's known bad habits and ways by ignoring the fact that those bad behavioral patterns have become firmly ingrained in a person as a matter of routine over time, and are therefore extremely difficult to undo. And yet, they may only represent bad-habit laziness in most cases, such as not cleaning the sink of toothpaste after brushing their teeth, or leaving the sink full of dirty dishes after a meal. When it comes to deeply held convictions (or delusions), however, these are much harder to overturn. That is why God commanded Israel not to intermarry with the heathen tribes they were conquering— "For they will turn away thy son from following me, that they may serve other gods" (Deuteronomy 7:4). Therefore, marrying a known unbeliever is disobedience to God. The strong bonds that form between Christian couples, through shared spiritual experiences such as praying daily and attending church weekly, are never formed if only one partner is involved in those activities. In fact, the spirituality of the believer often comes under assault by the unbeliever, forcing the believer to choose between God and the marriage partner. Matthew Henry astutely observed "there is more reason to fear that the bad will corrupt the good than to hope that the good will reform the bad, as there is in laying two pears together, the one rotten and the other sound."[47] The passions of the heart can be unpredictable and frivolous, yet many yield completely to its unsteady guidance. It is therefore necessary for the mind to overrule the heart—when it comes to consideration of a long-term relationship incompatible with the Word of God—and to govern with decisions made through wisdom, and not passion.

---

47 Henry, *Commentary*. Vol. 2, 103.

It should be noted that within a marriage of atheists, sometimes one partner may become converted by the Spirit. Since the marriage was made when *both* were yet unbelievers, it does not violate the commandment not to be yoked with unbelievers, which applies to a believer willingly marrying an unbeliever. Is that union unholy then, because of the unbeliever? St. Paul addresses that situation in one of his epistles: "For the unbelieving husband is sanctified by the wife, and the unbelieving wife is sanctified by the husband: else were your children unclean; but now are they holy" (1 Corinthians 7:14). As long as the unbeliever is not actively trying to subvert the faith of the believer, then the marriage is still blessed.

In all matters regarding love and marriage, it is imperative to remember that Satan desires the destruction of both. His influence in this world is diminished when we love and support each other through a godly union; "And if one prevail against him, two shall withstand him; and a threefold cord is not quickly broken" (Ecclesiastes 4:12). He seeks to put those bonds asunder through any means possible. Knowing this, we can survive marital problems by identifying the real enemy as Satan, and not as each other. We should then unite against that common enemy and seek to root out all of the subtle propaganda causing division in our relationships. The blustering winds of marital discontent should inspire us to wrap ourselves ever more firmly in coats of marital fidelity and harmony.

13

Business and Industry

Satan is active in all aspects of our lives, but possibly none more covertly than in our business affairs. After the fall of humanity in the Garden of Eden, God commanded us all to *earn* a living to survive; "In the sweat of thy face shalt thou eat bread, till thou return unto the ground" (Genesis 3:19). For those who are single, time can be divided almost equally between work and pleasure—working as little or as much as desired either just to get by, or to prosper—nevertheless, we must all work. "He becometh poor that dealeth *with* a slack hand: but the hand of the diligent maketh rich" (Proverbs 10:4). If the personal choice is to raise a family, however, then that need to earn becomes compounded into the driving force of life by having to take care of others in addition to oneself. It is because of that familial priority that some people will justify any manner of industry including, unfortunately, the deceitful or criminal.

I'm reminded of two scenes from the 1972 movie *The Godfather,* from the book written by Mario Puzo. In the first, Don Corleone is meeting with heroin dealer Virgil Sollozzo who is seeking financial backing and political protection. Corleone declines Sollozzo by explaining that dealing drugs is a dirty business which can lead to violence, and that he can't afford that kind of notoriety amongst the politicians in his back pocket or they'll abandon him. He then, however, immediately adds that he doesn't care what a man does for a living, as if it's all justifiable in providing for your family. Do people really want to try and legitimize, before the throne of eternal judgment, their participation in violent, criminal enterprises—when there were lawful occupational alternatives that could have been chosen instead?

"Better *is* a little with righteousness than great revenues without right" (Proverbs 16:8). Satisfying wealth comes from serving God through *honest* industry.

The other scene is when Michael Corleone is in church for the baptism of his child and renouncing Satan and all his works—all the while he's having his business competition murdered. Though obviously a drastic fictional scenario written for maximum impact, many people in real situations live under similar though less dramatic hypocrisy by making an outward show of piety in attending church every Sunday, but then returning on Monday to deceptive business practices just to make a quick, easy buck. "Dishonest money dwindles away, but whoever gathers money little by little makes it grow" (Proverbs 13:11, NIV). The mindset that we can *separate religion from business* to justify an unrighteousness manner of earning a living comes from Satan, whose underlying desire is to *separate religion from humanity*. He achieves this in great part through sowing seeds of materialism, discontent, laziness, and greed.

The materialistic desire for ever more possessions is the sin of coveting, disguised as healthy economic consumerism. We justify the desire for those things (the latest technology, expensive cars, huge homes, trendy fashion accessories, etc.) by telling ourselves that we *need* them, when, in fact, most of humanity throughout history has done quite well without them—as could we too at this current moment. When luxuries become redefined as necessities to be obtained, we know that Satan is filling our minds with an unhealthy desire which can be summed up in the bumper sticker slogan "He who dies with the most toys wins." Unfortunately, he who lives and dies guided by that philosophy is a guaranteed *loser*. Consumerism leads to sinful pride manifested through the mindset that one has to "keep up with the Joneses" just to boast of socio-economic and cultural parity. It is then that we need to remind ourselves of what Jesus taught us: "And he said unto them, Take heed, and beware of covetousness: for a man's life consisteth not in the abundance of the things which he possesseth" (Luke 12:15). It is okay to have some of the "toys" in life designed to make life easier or more comfortable, but an unquenchable desire always for *more* shows a distrust in

God's willingness to provide. "But my God shall supply all your need according to his riches in glory by Christ Jesus" (Philippians 4:19). More importantly, it also reveals that we have made a god of material possessions and physical comforts in this temporary life—superseding the spiritual values and rewards of the next life in the eternal presence of the one true God.

Discontent is a sin when it is the byproduct of resentment and envy. Spiritual discontent which drives us to become ever more holy is a good thing, but when we lose focus on the spiritual world to come, and instead focus on what others may have materially in this world over us, we have taken our eyes off the everlasting prize. "For what shall it profit a man, if he shall gain the whole world, and lose his own soul?" (Mark 8:36). If we have been graced with salvation through faith in Jesus Christ as the Son of God, our sins are pardoned and we are granted access to heaven. We have then won life's lottery. What temporary earthly monetary payout can match heavenly eternal bliss?

Discontentment also shows distrust in God and in His plan for us by implying that the Lord has somehow made a mistake in our lives when, in fact, the only mistake is in our misguided perception of the circumstances. St. Paul has written about the secret to contentment in Philippians 4:11–13—"Not that I speak in respect of want: for I have learned, in whatsoever state I am, *therewith* to be content. I know both how to be abased, and I know how to abound: every where and in all things I am instructed both to be full and to be hungry, both to abound and to suffer need. I can do all things through Christ which strengtheneth me." Furthermore, his epistle has provided a battle strategy against succumbing to worldly discontent; "Finally, brethren, whatsoever things are true, whatsoever things *are* honest, whatsoever things *are* just, whatsoever things *are* pure, whatsoever things *are* lovely, whatsoever things *are* of good report; if *there be* any virtue, and if *there be* any praise, think on these things" (Philippians 4:8). When we have eliminated general discontent in our lives, we can also eliminate the specific financial discontent that drives us to accumulate wealth at any cost—especially through the corruption of our business and industry.

Laziness leads people to taking shortcuts on the job, which are often illegal, rather than exercising diligence in doing business uprightly and by the book. It robs us of personal satisfaction by not fulfilling all of our work responsibilities to ourselves and others. Procrastination leads to work pile-up, which leads to greater stress, and possibly to taking even greater shortcuts or to the complete abandonment of certain duties. "Go to the ant, thou sluggard; consider her ways, and be wise: Which having no guide, overseer, or ruler, Provideth her meat in the summer, *and* gathereth her food in the harvest" (Proverbs 6:6-8). Being unproductive is self-defeating and could lead to eventual firing, or personal business collapse through fines, sanctions, or lost revenue.

Greed reveals an idolatrous love of money over God and others. Those consumed by it are miserable creatures. For them, the *end-all* of money is to acquire and hoard it, instead of seeing it as a *means to an end* to be spent on comforts and necessities. The focus is shifted onto the *tool* and away from the tool's *purpose*. And when the purpose of it does inevitably arise, and people are forced to spend it—even for household *necessities* such as food, heating, or electricity—the greedy reveal their miserly torment and become resentful. They oftentimes convert and project their self-inflicted psychological suffering into physical suffering upon those around them by limiting the basics. The home is freezing in the winter because they won't turn up the heat—forcing everyone inside to huddle in blankets and sweatshirts just to keep warm as if they were all living outside the home. Or, they refuse to use the air-conditioning in sweltering heat, endangering the elderly amongst them. Frequently, the household grocery list is not filled with any specific wants or desires, but only with items bought at a reduced price through coupons. Now, for families living around the poverty level, those austere measures are wise and necessary implementations. But for families that are well off, greed can force unnecessary restrictions which deny the Lord's bounty, and force people to live life less abundantly than God is graciously providing. Greed also denies charitable giving to others. "Then said Jesus unto his disciples, Verily I say unto you, That a rich man shall hardly enter into the kingdom of heaven" (Matthew 19:23). Unlike other vices such as gluttony and lust which can be temporarily sated, "He that loveth silver shall not be satisfied with silver; nor he that loveth abundance with increase" (Ecclesiastes 5:10). There is always an unquenchable desire for more, even though it has been shown that once the basic needs of life are met, having more money on top of that does *not* lead to any greater happiness.

Greed is manifested not just in consumption or accumulation, but in productivity as well. Working far beyond meeting the needs of the family as a "workaholic" is a facet of greed many people overlook as simple exuberance for their occupation. While it is true that some people either do have a great passion for their work or may need to work excessive hours to meet their financial needs, those "engaged workers" are not classic workaholics.

The all-consuming passion of the workaholic to earn has been shown to be pathological in most cases because of its high potential for negative consequences which take a toll on marriage and the family by creating an absent father in the home. According to Malissa A. Clark, PhD, workaholism decreases job satisfaction, family satisfaction/functioning, life satisfaction, and physical, emotional, and mental health—while increasing job stress, counterproductive work behaviors, marital disaffection, work-life conflict, overall burnout, emotional exhaustion, cynicism, and depersonalization.[48] It is an unhealthy addiction justified by many people as a way to further their career prospects in order to help their family from without—while it simultaneously destroys their family from within.

The disordered love of riches often leads to cheating and double-dealing with others in the affairs of business. The unwritten laws of supply and demand might govern a free economy, yet even they have some moral and legal limitations. For example, price gouging in emergency situations to take advantage of people in need after a catastrophic event is not only a crime in most states; it is a sin because it defies the law of God which commands that "Thou shalt not defraud thy neighbour, neither rob *him*" (Le-

---

48 Clark, Malissa A., PhD. "Workaholism: It's Not Just Long Hours on the Job." *Psychological Science Agenda* 30, no. 4 (April 2016). Accessed June 6, 2018. http://www.apa.org/science/about/psa/2016/04/workaholism.aspx.

viticus 19:13). Also, "A false balance *is* abomination to the LORD: but a just weight *is* his delight" (Proverbs 11:1). Willfully profiting from others' misery stands in defiance of Jesus' command that "Thou shalt love thy neighbour as thyself" (Mark 12:31). Taking advantage of crises, cheating, and double-dealing in business are all forms of stealing—the most prevalent crime in the workplace.

However, stealing by employers through unscrupulous business practices is still not as widespread as stealing by employees. Employee theft is so prevalent because it is covered under a multitude of sins. Whether falsifying mileage reports for greater reimbursement, abusing the petty cash expenditures, using the company stamping machine for personal mail, making long-distance personal phone calls on the company's dime, taking home stationery and other office supplies for home use, showing up late for work, taking extended breaks or meals, watching social media videos during work hours, engaging in social media chatting, or sending and receiving personal texts throughout the business day—these are all examples of stealing from your employer. Some may involve the actual theft of physical cash, while others involve the theft of goods and services. What is likely to be the greatest expense to businesses—costing billions of dollars in lost productivity worldwide—is the theft of time. If you're on the clock and being paid to work, and you're deliberately not working, you're stealing. Satan has made an inroad into your character and behavior that may seem slight to you, but can have larger eternal consequences because little sins add up. Judas Iscariot did not set out to betray our Lord. But while he was in charge of the moneybag, Scripture notes that he became accustomed to stealing from it, (see John 12:6). Routinely robbing from the group's petty cash is what set Judas on the greedy road to obtaining thirty pieces of silver by selling out the Christ. Jesus warned us that "whoever is dishonest with very little will also be dishonest with much" (Luke 16:10, NIV). The way of sin is downhill. One sin leads to more and greater sins.

Nor is it enough to avoid cheating and stealing in business to avert a divine retribution. We must also not enter into an unholy alliance with Satan by working a job that may be legal, yet one that promotes his agenda. Medical doctors are esteemed for their skills at healing, and swear an oath to do no harm. Why, then, would any doctor choose to work in an abortion clinic routinely taking innocent lives? Those doctors need to ask themselves as did Job: "Did not he who made me in the womb make them? Did not the same one form us both within our mothers?" (Job 31:15, NIV). Working as a hotel clerk is a respectable job, unless you choose to do so at a sleazy hotel advertising hourly rates to promote prostitution. Those doing so may even "profess that they know God; but in works they deny *him*, being abominable, and disobedient, and unto every good work reprobate" (Titus 1:16). Most people claim that they have a novel in them they'd love to write. Should they do so if it merely becomes an exercise in penning perverse eroticism? If that's the case, "Examine yourselves, whether ye be in the faith; prove your own selves" (2 Corinthians 13:5). Write something uplifting and enlightening instead, if you can, or don't write anything at all. Is a filmmaker who specializes in pornography contributing anything positive to humanity, or simply acting as Satan's agent in tempting us to sin according to scriptural warnings? "But every man is tempted, when he is drawn away of his own lust, and enticed" (James 1:14). Retailing is a perfectly legitimate profession, unless we open a shop to sell items and books promoting Satanism and the occult. Then, "Cursed *shall be* thy basket and thy store" (Deuteronomy 28:17). What of musicians who use their music to promote race-hatred and bigotry, distrust of police, or violence against women? The Bible tells us how to regard them: "Now I beseech you, brethren, mark them which cause divisions and offences contrary to the doctrine which ye have learned; and avoid them" (Romans 16:17). Do not consume their rotten fruit, nor produce it yourselves.

Even a noble, *once-neutral* profession such as teaching, can be corrupted away from education into indoctrination of an ideological agenda instead. When the three R's of reading, 'riting, and 'rithmetic are replaced with revisionism, regurgitation, and revolution, then the practitioners have become *ignoble* by robbing a generation of students of the necessary educational tools and skills they will need to survive in this competitive world.

In all that we do in our business and industry, whether as owner or employee, we need to score the job to see whether or not it comports to the will of God in our lives. "And whatsoever ye do, do *it* heartily, as to the Lord, and not unto men" (Colossians 3:23). If the job brings glory to the Lord through ministrations or beneficial services to our brethren, then it's a desirable profession in the eyes of the Lord. And though not many are blessed to serve the Lord directly through their occupations, those working everyday jobs that are spiritually neutral can still demonstrate Christian principles of brotherly love through their interactions with coworkers and/or the public which will redound to the glory of the Lord. "A *good* name *is* rather to be chosen than great riches, *and* loving favour rather than silver and gold" (Proverbs 22:1). On the other hand, if the job lays stumbling blocks which hinder spiritual growth in yourself or in others, if it contributes to the detriment of your soul through anger and hatred, or if it leaves you feeling hopeless and futile, then it is an occupation to be avoided at all costs. Pray to seek other work, and you shall find it.

14

Interpersonal Relationships

Humans are social beings. When God created Adam, He also created a partner for him in Eve because it was "not good that the man should be alone" (Genesis 2:18). They then built families, communities, and eventually peopled the world with nations. It is in our nature to seek the company of others and to form relationships with them for personal satisfaction as well as for survival.

The main types of relationships generally involve family, friends, love, and business. Because more than one person is involved, all relationships are a two-way street, requiring a delicate balance between give and take for it to succeed as a benefit to the participants. It's within that process of mutual concession and compromise where Satan has his greatest opportunity to sow seeds of division—for he knows that "... if one prevail against him, two shall withstand him ..." (Ecclesiastes 4:12). We truly are stronger united than divided.

We've already seen the benefits of marriage to the family unit in Chapter Twelve of this work, and of how Satan seeks to put asunder that which God has joined together. Not content with driving a wedge between husband and wife, he attempts to divide the other members within the nuclear family as well by fostering sibling rivalries. Generally (depending upon the age of the child), the first seeds are sown in firstborn children when they learn that there is a second child on the way. A jealous fear of losing their parents' full attention seizes them, and resentment is firmly implanted. When the new baby is brought home, and much time and attention is necessarily bestowed upon the helpless infant, the firstborn begins to compete for time and attention. This may manifest itself through negative acting out over what is seen as unfair and preferential treatment afforded the infant. In extreme cases, the elder child may even seek physically to harm the younger sibling. (Cain killed Abel over God's favored regard for Abel's sacrifice—see Genesis 4:8.) As the latter-born children grow, they may experience a selfish unwillingness on the part of their older sibling to share toys or playtime, and may become victims of bullying—thereby ensuring that the seeds of anger and resentment germinated in the first-born become dispersed into the fertile ground of the second-born sibling as well. Then the cycle may be repeated in the second-born through their treatment of subsequent children. Thus the pecking order is firmly established, thereby creating the potential for lifelong family animosity in some—dependent upon the severity of the "pecking." It is therefore important for parents to salt the fields of jealousy and resentment so that Satan cannot sow those seeds in the older sibling. One particularly effective method is for parents to bestow a position of favored importance to the older child, by charging that child with the love and protection of the new sibling. "Behold, how good and how pleasant *it is* for brethren to dwell together in unity!" (Psalm 133:1). Teach them to be teachers and guides, and they will serve their parents and their siblings eagerly.

Outside the nuclear family, Satan is also active in dividing members of the extended family. As there is usually much less contact between extended family members than between nuclear family members, there is a greater opportunity for Satan to sow long-term resentments, prejudices, and jealousies; dealing with those negative issues does not require the same immediacy as would be so within the nuclear family to maintain household harmony.

We often see resentment between the children of siblings living under disparate socioeconomic conditions. If, for example, a sister becomes a successful plastic surgeon while her brother remains an unknown struggling musician, then the ground is fertile for Satan to sow seeds of arrogant superiority in the children of the sister while sowing seeds of discontent, jealousy, or resentment in the children of the brother. The pampered children living in a Beverly Hills mansion may look down upon their cousins living hand to mouth in a confined, rented apartment, and treat them disdainfully. Likewise, the impoverished children may resent their cousins' prosperity and develop a resentful and hostile jealousy towards them in return. Satan will water those fields relentlessly to germinate resentment.

We often see Satan active in exaggerating cultural and religious differences to invoke prejudices and stoke age-old animosities. Marrying someone outside their ethnicity can create problems for many throughout the extended family. Arabs and Jews who marry, for example, may experience cultural pressure from both their extended families. Jews and Gentiles who marry may experience religious pressure as well. Satan counts on blind hatred begetting more blind hatred. Scripture tells us however that while "Hatred stirreth up strifes ... love covereth all sins" (Proverbs 10:12). Only love can conquer hate. If we're aware of the root causes, we can *uproot* them and break that vicious cycle.

Sometimes even grandparents become alienated from their grandchildren by their own cultural biases and preferences for the earlier "better" times. They are reluctant to accept that everything changes, and they forget how, in their day, their own social practices were likely criticized and condemned as radical departures from societal norms as well. They indirectly denounce the younger generation through a combination of fear of the future, and ignorance of the past. They (wittingly or unwittingly) create an often-insurmountable generation gap by criticizing them through their nostalgic longing for the past. In those instances, they need to be reminded of Scripture which warns: "Say not thou, What is *the cause* that the former days were better than these? for thou dost not inquire wisely concerning this" (Ecclesiastes 7:10). Every generation thinks that its own is the best, oftentimes focusing selectively on the few pluses while ignoring the many minuses. Old dogs *can* learn new tricks if they are willing to try.

We see personal jealousies acted out in the classic mother-in-law problem, wherein the two women—mother and wife—seem to compete for the son/husband's affections and allegiances. Though the Bible clearly states "Therefore shall a man leave his father and his mother, and shall cleave unto his wife: and they shall be one flesh" (Genesis 2:24), it is hard for many mothers to relinquish priority in their child's life—especially if it's their only child—to see it bestowed upon another person in their place. Satan exploits that situation through instilling fear, anxiety, and resentment in mothers about losing love and influence in their child's life. Parents who fall prey to his deception forget that the Lord also commanded children to "Honour thy father and thy mother: that thy days may be long upon the land which the LORD thy God giveth thee" (Exodus 20:12). Therefore, "Train up a child in the way he should go: and when he is old, he will not depart from it" (Proverbs 22:6). Cutting the apron strings will not result in severing the love bonds between parents and children, if they are brought up according to biblical tenets.

Friendships are another favorite target of Satan's arrows because bonds of self-sacrificial friendship are oftentimes stronger than family fellowships vulnerable to sibling rivalries. "A friend loveth at all times, and a brother is born for adversity" (Proverbs 17:17). We see perfect examples in Scripture of godly friendship between David and Jonathan—"... that the soul of Jonathan was knit with the soul of David, and Jonathan loved him as his own soul" (1 Samuel 18:1)—and with Elisha who said to Elijah, "*As* the LORD liveth, and *as* thy soul liveth, I will not leave thee" (2 Kings 2:2). And there are other references, too. Devoted friendships transcend worldly obstacles.

Primatologists have defined friendship as a "long-term, positive relationship that involves cooperation."[49] This is established through self-disclosure and reciprocity. It is emotionally satisfying to know that a friend will stand by you in times of trouble or emotional turmoil, no matter what. It is a proven fact that we stand stronger together with others than we do standing alone. This is exactly why Satan seeks to break the bonds of friendship. He roams the earth as a prowling lion seeking to separate individuals from the herd. A firm grounding in Scripture reassures us that we are never alone, for Jesus said "I am with you always, even to the end of the age" (Matthew 28:20). However, in these

---

49 Seyfarth, Robert M., and Dorothy L. Cheney. "The evolutionary origins of friendship." Annual review of psychology 63 (2012): 153-177. https://web-facstaff.sas.upenn.edu/~seyfarth/Publications/annurev-psych-%20Friendship.pdf

end times filled with hostility towards any religious teaching or expression, that firm spiritual grounding in the faith and knowledge of a constant Companion is lost so that once friendships are broken, people are left with nothing but empty loneliness. When people are cut off from the emotional reinforcement of others, they are more vulnerable to Satan's further deceptions. It is in that fertile ground that he can plant seeds of hopelessness and despair. We are seeing the fruits of those malignant efforts with a 30 percent increase of suicides in the United States since 1999.[50] In 2017, Americans died in record numbers to alcohol, drugs, and suicides combined—twice as many as in 1999.[51]

Many of the devil's devices employed in sabotaging loving relationships have already been explored under *Love and Marriage* (Chapter Twelve). There are a few additional root causes that should be identified as well. Revelation 9:11 (NIV) describes Satan as "the angel of the Abyss, whose name in Hebrew is Abaddon and in Greek is Apollyon (that is, Destroyer)." Not only does he attempt to destroy loving unions through external means such as financial stress, sexual temptation, etc., but he is also very subtle in fostering patterns of self-sabotage internally, of which many people are not even aware. Personal insecurity and doubt comes from Satan. It is one of the greatest weapons in his arsenal to destroy relationships. That critical "inner voice" that tears you down instead of building you up does not come from the Holy Spirit. "For God hath not given us the spirit of fear; but of power, and of love, and of a sound mind" (2 Timothy 1:7). That whispering you may hear—filling you with fear that your mate doesn't find you attractive anymore; that you're not smart enough; or caring enough, etc.—comes from Satan. Ignore it.

Personal insecurity in a relationship manifests itself in many ways. An inability to properly process constructive criticism is one sure indicator, and often leads to defensive overreactions. Do

---

50 Suicides rates up 30% in United States since 1999. "Morbidity and Mortality Weekly Report (MMWR)." Centers for Disease Control and Prevention. June 07, 2018. Accessed June 08, 2018. https://www.cdc.gov/mmwr/volumes/67/wr/mm6722a1.htm?s_cid=mm6722a1_x.

51 Musumeci, Natalie, and Natalie Musumeci. "Record Number of Americans Died from Alcohol, Drugs and Suicide in 2017." New York Post. March 05, 2019. Accessed March 09, 2019. https://nypost.com/2019/03/05/record-number-of-americans-died-from-alcohol-drugs-and-suicide-in-2017/.

you find yourself keeping secrets from your mate because you are either afraid of being harshly judged, or because you value tact over honesty? Do you feel that you have to sacrifice your individuality and adopt identical thoughts and actions as your partner, in order to be accepted? Then you need to remember that "There is no fear in love; but perfect love casteth out fear: because fear hath torment. He that feareth is not made perfect in love" (1 John 4:18). You are who you are, and your partner has accepted you already. Don't allow sudden floods of satanic doubt to undermine that rock-solid foundation and wash away all that you've built up together.

Conversely, do you think that changing your partner's ways into matching your own will create a more solid relationship? It won't. Does personal laziness result in your increasingly saying no to requests for assistance in sharing the workload? If so, how long do you think it will it be before your partner finally gets fed up with carrying all of the weight and calls it quits? Greatest of all destroyers is the inability to forgive. If you cannot let go of grievances and choose to build resentment over them instead, then you are sabotaging your relationship incident upon incident.

The workplace is another key terrain Satan seizes upon to assault relationships, since we spend a good portion of our lives at work building associations with others. Workplace relationships generally fall under two basic categories—professional or personal—though there may be some overlap between them. Professional relationships are transactional, and focus on one's work or career. They usually involve either a superior/subordinate structure, or an equal cooperative arrangement between coworkers and team members. In contrast, personal relationships are for social satisfaction at the workplace and involve building friendships designed to offer shared support through the daily grind of the business day. Properly nurtured, both types of relationships are mutually beneficial between participants, and as such, both become principal targets for assault by Satan.

One of the greatest openings for Satan to exploit is in the disparity of power and influence between employer and employee. The one who can be fired is at the mercy of the one who can fire. The one who can promote can coerce the one who seeks promotion. This unequal arrangement has the potential for great abuses. An intimidating work environment can produce relationships more akin to those of master/slave than of employer/employee if workers are compelled to perform jobs outside their official capacity in the company. Harassment isn't limited to performance/reward (*quid pro quo*) arrangements either. Offensive jokes, racial and ethnic slurs, insults and ridicule, all create a hostile work environment legally constituting harassment. The most common form of harassment we've seen recently exposed is sexual. The #MeToo movement has brought into the light many of the dark dealings that have occurred behind closed doors. Thirty-three million women claim to have been sexually harassed in the workplace, according to an ABC News-Washington Post poll.[52] Though most commonly reported, sexual harassment is not limited to males preying upon females. Female bosses also have harassed male employees. Same-sex sexual harassments occur as well. The common factor is the power inequality that enables predators to seek prey. "Be sober, be vigilant; because your adversary the devil, as a roaring lion, walketh about, seeking whom he may devour" (1 Peter 5:8). It is important to identify immediately any improper speech or conduct which creates discomfort, and eliminate it before it can metastasize into something greater which may cause lifelong personal or professional damage.

    Work ethics between coworking individuals will naturally vary and therefore should not be brought into comparison. Expecting others to replicate your own perceived "good" attitudes toward work will only result in resentment, anger, and frustration on your part if you judge their work ethics as deficient or substandard to your own. "Judge not, that ye be not judged" (Matthew 7:1). If others' work ethics are truly unsatisfactory, that is an issue for the boss to address. The chances are pretty high that inadequate employees would have been fired already in the private business sector, where the bottom line is profit and productivity. In the public sector—where strong municipal unions may protect the lazy, indolent worker—focus instead on your

---

52 Langer, Gary. "Unwanted Sexual Advances Not Just a Hollywood, Weinstein Story, Poll Finds." ABC News. October 17, 2017. Accessed July 01, 2018. https://abcnews.go.com/Politics/unwanted-sexual-advances-hollywood-weinstein-story-poll/story?id=50521721.

own efforts and achievements and don't worry about how others apply (or don't apply) themselves. "Whatever you do, work at it with all your heart, as working for the Lord, not for human masters, since you know that you will receive an inheritance from the Lord as a reward. It is the Lord Christ you are serving" (Colossians 3:23-24, NIV). God sees and rewards diligence in all good things accordingly, whether or not anyone else does.

Negative work ethics are simply a manifestation of negative life attitudes. The lazy person at home will likely be the unproductive procrastinator at work. "One who is slack in his work is brother to one who destroys" (Proverbs 18:9, NIV). The person inconsiderate of others' punctuality—who routinely shows up late for social gatherings—will likely be the one consistently punching in late at work. Those, along with all the other bad habits we may have developed, were fostered by Satan to sow discord in our personal lives. In our professional lives, those bad habits translate into frustrated productivity and hindered cohesion with others.

Other weapons Satan uses to divide people at work include jealousy, resentment, paranoia, and fear. The system of raises and promotions can create jealousy in those overlooked, who feel more deserving than those rewarded. Comparing workloads, salaries, or bonuses creates stagnant pools for resentment to fester in. Productive employees may create paranoia and fear in those directly over them managerially by appearing to be vying for their jobs. In extreme cases, this could result in the manager eliminating the perceived threat by unfairly undermining the innocently industrious employee.

One particularly insidious way Satan destroys relationships at the workplace is through the use of gossip. What transpires privately between two people at the water cooler may create far-reaching ripples that shipwreck the lives or careers of others. Because of the potential for devastation, office gossip has been likened to workplace violence. "A perverse person stirs up conflict, and a gossip separates close friends" (Proverbs 16:28, NIV). Long-term chronic gossip at the workplace results in reduced morale and trust, coupled with increased anxiety and division. Immediate, acute reactions to gossip could include the breakup of marriages through misrepresentations of platonic professional male-female interactions, or professionally result in demotions or firing of employees. "Set a watch, O LORD, before my mouth; keep the door of my lips" (Psalm 141:3). Be on your guard both against entertaining gossip, and furthering it.

Sometimes, events at work can create negative false perceptions that carry forward into lifelong personal attitudes. If you were justly fired from a job because you hardly ever bothered to show up for work, the firing wasn't due to anything but absenteeism. Raising allegations of sexual bias or racism to explain it are almost always excuses to gloss over personal ineptitude. An employer shouldn't be forced to pay wages to an absentee employee. It's that simple. Yet, Satan uses that situation to foster divisions. Own up to your shortcomings and take responsibility for your actions. Then purge your bad work habits and enjoy a satisfying and prosperous career.

Interpersonal relationships between men and women, family and friends, bosses and coworkers, are all prime targets for destruction by the enemy of humanity. Don't allow his divisive propaganda to gain a foothold in any of those relationships "Lest Satan should get an advantage of us: for we are not ignorant of his devices" (2 Corinthians 2:11). Identifying his malicious deceit in all its manifestations will deter his agenda to divide us.

15

Politics

Perhaps the two most contentious issues in the history of the world—possessing the greatest potential for creating strife and division—are religion and politics. No other topics have caused more collective grief and suffering than these two combined. Religious and political disagreements have resulted in heretic-inquisitional mass murder as well as international wars. The religious divisions sown by Satan to sever personal connections to God have been discussed throughout this work. Because politics is the civic arena in which the spiritual war between God and Satan is waged throughout society, it is now time to address the root causes of political divisions in a nation and to discover that they, too, are Satanic in origin.

Without assigning blame to any single political party by name—as there are many inter-party crossover issues—it is better to judge each political plank in any party's platform by the Word of God so that you can decide for yourself. First American President, George Washington (1732–1799), noted in his 1796 farewell speech that "... reason and experience both forbid us to expect that national morality can prevail in exclusion of religious principle." Because the Bible is the ultimate guide to morality and godliness, let us dig deep into each contentious social issue and see how it relates to Scripture. That is the only true measure to use in deciding to accept or reject a political position, regardless of one's current political affiliation.

Obviously, Satan isn't going to come right out and declare his intentions to destroy civilization. Instead, he masks those designs under a veneer of justice, equality, and fraternity. "And no marvel; for Satan himself is transformed into an angel of light"

(2 Corinthians 11:14). His evil agenda of division is promoted under the guise of good intentions—regardless of the contradictory results. In these days of politically correct, hyper-emotional responses to many media-manufactured crises, it is easy to succumb to a false empathy. Many of today's political movements are misguided responses to Satan's deceitful emotional ploys. Not coincidentally, many of those political movements also happen to drive us further from God as a nation, and from each other, as fellow citizens. That is Satan's design, and it needs to be uncovered to keep a nation from being led down the path of ruin.

A good place to start deconstructing Satan's political platform is in the study of the Ten Commandments given to Moses by God on Mount Sinai, (listed here in order according to the Protestant King James Version which differs slightly from the Roman Catholic version of the commandments). A nation that rejects those commandments is a nation that forfeits God's blessings. "... [K]now therefore and see that *it is* an evil *thing* and bitter, that thou hast forsaken the LORD thy God, and that my fear *is* not in thee, saith the Lord GOD of hosts" (Jeremiah 2:19). "Those who honor me I will honor, but those who despise me will be disdained" (1 Samuel 2:30, NIV). We need only look to the history of the Israelites in the Old Testament—whenever they backslid into idolatry—to see the awful consequences of rejecting God and His commandments.

THE FIRST COMMANDMENT STATES, "I *am* the LORD thy God, which have brought thee out of the land of Egypt, out of the house of bondage. Thou shalt have no other gods before me" (Exodus 20:2-3). However, today's rage by secular activists against any public expression of personal religion—advanced judicially under the phony "separation of church and state" doctrine—has hindered or prevented the establishment of God's sovereignty in the lives of many through intimidation, thereby nullifying the commandment so as to allow the worship of all manner of secular gods according to one's particular affections. Some people materialistically worship money. Others hedonistically worship pleasure. And still others narcissistically worship themselves through an inflated ego. In politics, the three major false gods I will address here are government, animals, and the environment.

For many, Big Government has become their god. They look to the politician's arm of flesh to protect them instead of trusting in the Almighty arm of God. It is no wonder, then, that many end up beaten by that arm of flesh they entrusted to protect them. Under an excessively large government, the arbitrary rule of man usurps God's immutable rule of law. Inalienable rights bestowed upon all by the Creator are now bestowed selectively by the government—upon favored political allies and constituencies. Additional human "rights" are then imparted to members of special-interest groups through quotas and set-asides—usually by judicial fiat and *not* by the will of the people as expressed through the legislative bodies of a representative government. When people are enticed to trade away personal freedoms and autonomy for the ease and comfort of "free stuff" and the attainment of special privileges through their votes, then the benefits received have become nothing less than payment of bribes.

American polymath Benjamin Franklin (1706–1790) warned, "When the people find that they can vote themselves money, that will herald the end of the republic." The deviousness of that political cunning, however, is lost on those supporting that type of *quid pro quo* exchange—as the masses of people react emotionally instead of logically. Public social welfare, for example, was designed to be a temporary hand-*up*, and not a permanent hand-*out*. Its intent was to help people over temporary financial bumps and potholes, and not meant to pave the road of life ahead for them. Paul the Apostle wrote in 2 Thessalonians 3:10 "... that if any would not work, neither should he eat." Yet for too many people, political sentiment nullifies reason. Thinking they are doing immediate good by voting for those who give away free money, food, housing, etc., they don't see the long-term harm of creating multi-generational helplessness and dependency. Instead of assisting the achievement of self-sufficiency, they promote a lifelong government dependency, thereby enslaving people on bureaucratic welfare plantations.

Unfortunately, this is exactly the intended result of some in the ruling class—to create dependency—and then promise satisfaction under the stipulation that they can only deliver while *they* remain in power because the political opposition will cruelly end their welfare life support, if elected. To maintain that power to redistribute the wealth of others, they need the habitual votes of those people they've made to feel helpless. To retain their votes during political campaigns, they need to cultivate a sense of victimization. And so they engage in brutal fearmongering about the opposition party through the use of hysterical hyperbole. How many election cycles have we heard the same old tired mantras of politicians claiming their opponents are waging a war on women, or on children; or that they hate minorities; or they only give tax cuts to the rich; or that they want to poison the planet; or even intend to throw grandma off the cliff by ending her Medicare? Sowing class warfare by pitting citizen against citizen—men against women, race against race, rich against poor, young against old, etc.—is a classic divide-and-conquer strategy of Satan and should be rejected by those possessing any sense of religion, morality, or decency. Be on your guard against their false benevolence. It is not *your* welfare they care about, but their *own*. Allie Beth Stuckey notes that "Big government isn't intended to get the poor out of poverty. It's intended to keep them there. Continued dependency is the fuel on which big government runs."[53] Without dependents, there is no need for providers.

Other false gods include the worship of animals. Animism is "the belief that all natural things, such as plants, animals, rocks, and thunder, have spirits and can influence human events."[54] It is one thing to denounce the malicious or negligent treatment of animals. If we are not all doing so, there is no humanity within us. But it is quite another thing to elevate animal life over human life to the point where people think it's acceptable to set bombs that maim or kill people working in animal research laboratories. Sounds like an extreme misportrayal of an ideology? You decide. Read these quotes from leaders of groups boasting millions of members, who ratify that extreme position:

---

53 https://patriotpost.us/articles/56996-monday-short-cuts

54 "Animism Definition in the Cambridge English Dictionary." Cambridge Dictionary. Accessed July 06, 2018. https://dictionary.cambridge.org/us/dictionary/english/animism.

"In a war you have to take up arms and people will get killed, and I can support that kind of action by petrol bombing and bombs under cars, and probably at a later stage, the shooting of vivisectors on their doorsteps. It's a war, and there's no other way you can stop vivisectors."—Tim Daley, British Animal Liberation Front Leader.[55]

Former Director of People for the Ethical Treatment of Animals (PETA), Alex Pacheco, once stated that "Arson, property destruction, burglary and theft are 'acceptable crimes' when used for the animal cause." [56]

Michael W. Fox, Vice President of The Humane Society of the United States, once stated that "The life of an ant and that of my child should be granted equal consideration."[57]

Animal-rights activist and President of PETA, Ingrid Newkirk, once wrote that "A rat is a pig is a dog is a boy." Though she was comparing the animal nature of all creatures, the intent was to lower humans to the level of beasts, because she also said that "Six million Jews died in concentration camps, but six billion broiler chickens will die this year in slaughter houses," implying that the greater numbers reveal the greater crime.[58]

Equating the hateful genocidal Holocaust to the poultry industry supplying humanity with food is an extremely dangerous and misguided spiritual position to adopt. It completely denies the hierarchy established when "... God said, Let us make man in our image, after our likeness: and let them have dominion over the fish of the sea, and over the fowl of the air, and over the cattle, and over all the earth, and over every creeping thing that creepeth upon the earth" (Genesis 1:26). It also denies the divinity within human beings made in *God's image* by either denying the

---

55 See https://books.google.com/books?id=_6jfDQAAQBAJ&pg=PA73&dq=In+a+war+you+have+to+take+up+arms+and+people+will+get+killed,+and+I+can+support+that+kind+of+action+by+petrol+bombing&hl=en&sa=X&ved=0ahUKEwjDu_SFv_biAhUih-AKHRE0BV4Q6AEILzAB#v=onepage&q=In%20a%20war%20you%20have%20to%20

56 See https://newrepublic.com/article/76339/animal-spirits

57 See https://www.activistfacts.com/person/3365-michael-w-fox/

58 See https://www.jweekly.com/2005/05/20/this-time-peta-s-guilty-of-missing-the-point/

existence of the soul altogether, or by imputing it to all creatures, in contradiction to Scripture. God has granted us dominion over the flora and fauna of this world to use as we see fit for food, or clothing, or labor. Reducing humanity to an equal spiritual footing with the brute beasts denies the scriptural fact that only humans have an eternal soul. "What is man, that thou art mindful of him? or the son of man, that thou visitest him? Thou madest him a little lower than the angels; thou crownedst him with glory and honour, and didst set him over the works of thy hands" (Hebrews 2:6-7). Denying this hierarchical reality only leads to division, threats, hatred, and violence, as we've seen articulated above. This, too, comes from Satan.

Another great substitution for God can be seen in the radical environmental movement. Dr. Michael Crichton (1942-2008), renowned American author and screenwriter, observed the religious parallels between Judeo-Christian faith and environmentalism:

> There's an initial Eden, a paradise, a state of grace and unity with nature, there's a fall from grace into a state of pollution as a result of eating from the tree of knowledge, and as a result of our actions there is a judgment day coming for us all. We are all energy sinners, doomed to die, unless we seek salvation, which is now called sustainability. Sustainability is salvation in the church of the environment. Just as organic food is its communion, that pesticide-free wafer that the right people with the right beliefs, imbibe.[59]

The goddess of environmentalism is Gaia—Mother Earth. Many worship her to the exclusion of all else. While it is imperative to be good stewards of the planet and not to pollute and abuse it, it becomes an obsessive idolatry when the three R's of an academic education (reading, 'riting, and 'rithmetic) are supplanted by the three R's of environmentalism—reduce, reuse, and recycle. The recent prevalence of this dogmatic

---

59 Garreau, Joel. "Environmentalism as Religion." The New Atlantis. 2010. Accessed November 27, 2018. https://www.thenewatlantis.com/publications/environmentalism-as-religion.

teaching in our educational systems produces environmentally sensitive students who can build a compost heap, but unfortunately can't read their own diplomas.[60] Modern environmentalism demonizes *objective* science and capitalism, and threatens to punish those who don't accept their cherry-picked *subjective* "settled science." The result is the division of the country into adherents and deniers. When the deniers are threatened with violence, incarceration, or death because they skeptically take note of the myriad failed doomsday prophecies made by the climate-change movement, then you know Satan is actively agitating the debate. When naturally occurring, life-sustaining carbon dioxide gas is suddenly reclassified as a *pollutant*, then you know politics has also been injected into the debate.

As always with Satan, everything is a war. In the environmental movement, the war is on coal, carbon, fossil fuels, nuclear energy—all things that, when used responsibly, improve the lives of billions. People should not suffer wholesale for the appeasement of the non-existent goddess of the religion of environmentalism. The world should not be divided into two warring camps, especially when the actual (political) goal is simply income redistribution by any means necessary—including manufactured hysteria over global cooling (1970s), or global warming (1990s), or global climate change (currently)—all things which were accepted previously throughout history as weather patterns and cycles. Satan creates panic and hysteria, assigns blame, and therein divides us again.

The bottom line in practicing the first commandment is to determine whether or not you are allied to groups who worship false gods, usually through a shared political affiliation under one party's banner. The Bible warns us: "Be ye not unequally yoked together with unbelievers" (2 Corinthians 6:14). If you discover that you are, it's time to reconsider to whom you pledge your votes, and start voting for the principles of the Bible instead by recommitting your pledge to the one true God.

---

60 "Many Graduates Can't Read Their High School Diplomas." Tribunedigital-chicagotribune. April 23, 1987. Accessed July 06, 2018. http://articles.chicagotribune.com/1987-04-23/news/8701310386_1_assessment-and-program-evaluation-school-districts-adult-literacy-programs.

THE SECOND COMMANDMENT STATES "Thou shalt not make unto thee any graven image, or any likeness *of any thing* that *is* in heaven above, or that *is* in the earth beneath, or that *is* in the water under the earth" (Exodus 20:4). This commandment was intended to fortify Israel further against the idolatry forbidden in the first commandment when, in biblical times, it was common to carve gods out of gold and silver, wood and stone, and bow down before them in worship. Though this is not so common a practice today, we still see people praying to statues, pictures, and images. The point is that God is to be worshipped within the quietness of one's own soul, in the place where His Holy Spirit resides. "God *is* a Spirit: and they that worship him must worship *him* in spirit and in truth" (John 4:24). Internal belief needs no external representation or prompting to act.

There are other ways this commandment applies in our modern lives. Anything, in fact, that dominates our thoughts over thoughts of God and fills our time with wasteful activity over our time in worship, becomes idolatry. Obsessive use of technology is one particularly obvious example. "Americans check their phone on average once every 12 minutes—burying their heads in their phones 80 times a day, according to new research."[61] Other graven images people worship today are the golden calves of cars, homes, jewelry, and clothing, to name just a few. Certain hobbies and recreations can also constitute graven images when we carve out all of our time to accommodate them above all else. These are all distractions Satan uses to keep our focus off God. In global politics, there has been an extreme polarization of people toward parties of either the hard left or the hard right. The unbridgeable divisions between them—induced by Satan—have given rise to hatred and violence in many countries as each party worships the graven image of its party's standard. In America, those graven images are the donkey (Democrats) and the elephant (Republicans).

---

61 Swns. "Americans Check Their Phones 80 times a Day: Study." New York Post. November 08, 2017. Accessed July 07, 2018. https://nypost.com/2017/11/08/americans-check-their-phones-80-times-a-day-study/.

THE THIRD COMMANDMENT is one I see and hear violated repeatedly every single day; "Thou shalt not take the name of the LORD thy God in vain; for the LORD will not hold him guiltless that taketh his name in vain" (Exodus 20:7). We are to love and revere God; "For *as* the heavens are higher than the earth, so are my ways higher than your ways, and my thoughts than your thoughts" (Isaiah 55:9). Taking His name in vain shows a callous, sinful disregard for His exalted glory and honor. God must not be taken casually and reduced to lowly expressions of surprise or disbelief—as we see occurring repeatedly in texts sent between people containing the letters OMG, (Oh My God). The excessive, and apparently accepted use in society of this flippant reference to His grand majesty paves the way for even worse abuses, especially when OMG becomes coupled with profanity as in the horrific OMFG.

God's grandeur is further trodden upon by the profane use of the name of His Son. Though God "... highly exalted him, and given him a name which is above every name: That at the name of Jesus every knee should bow, of *things* in heaven, and *things* in earth, and *things* under the earth" (Philippians 2:9), the name of Jesus Christ is heard more commonly spoken today as a profanity. As noted previously in Chapter Three, watch any new movie out (above a general admission or family rating), and it seems that in order to get the movie produced, there must have been included in the contract, somewhere, that the name of Jesus Christ be used as an obscenity—with it usually appearing for the first time (of many) within five minutes of the movie's start. Long gone is the old Motion Picture Production Code (Hays Code) which set moral guidelines for the filmmaking industry. In fact, it has been turned so far around that the very concept of religious morality seems to be what is being censored, and all manner of abominations promoted instead. Did you ever notice in movies or in crime drama television shows how the characters that preach religion and spout Bible verses almost always turn out to be the psychotic murderers, rapists, kidnappers, or terrorists? Yet those who object to the mainstreaming of religion as deviancy, and who fight for the restoration of morality, are labeled as bigots, homophobes, and hate-mongers. It's now okay to blaspheme God, but anathema to blaspheme the blasphemers—free speech, tolerance, inclusion, and all that rubbish.

This shouldn't surprise us. Hollywood is well known for its decadence, debaucheries, and blasphemies. It's called "sin city" for a reason. To discover the political allies who aid and abet their attempts to define deviancy ever downward, just follow the money trail of candidate contributions and see who eagerly accepts their tainted money. Even the Pharisees of Jesus' time refused to accept back the thirty pieces of silver paid Judas Iscariot to betray our Lord—"And the chief priests took the silver pieces, and said, It is not lawful for to put them into the treasury, because it is the price of blood" (Matthew 27:6). Yet many politicians willingly and openly accept this *blood money* from known sexual harassers, molesters, rapists, pedophiles, drug addicts, and adulterers in the Hollywood community who overwhelmingly support one political party over the other—even to the point of expressing hatred of the opposing party at non-political award ceremonies meant to celebrate their own artistic accomplishments.

Furthermore, when the exalted name of God is deliberately removed from a party's political platform, and then is booed upon its restoration (though proposed solely for political expedience), the spiritual priorities of those delegates are made manifest for all to see. If you belong to that political party, then you cannot, in good conscience, call yourself a Christian by overlooking those blasphemies and keep voting for people who denounce any reference to, or inclusion of, God.

THE FOURTH COMMANDMENT reminds us to "Remember the sabbath day, to keep it holy. Six days shalt thou labour, and do all thy work ...." (Exodus 20:8–9). God made the heavens, the earth and all things upon it in six days, and rested on the seventh. We are to do likewise regarding labor and repose. The Sabbath is a day designated to recharge our spiritual batteries and fortify us for the week ahead. We need the mental rest in order to achieve spiritual growth.

For many, though, this commandment is challenged through financial necessity or emergency situations. Is it okay to work on the Sabbath to avoid foreclosure or bankruptcy? Is it okay to labor at home and dig out on Sunday, after a Saturday night snowstorm, so as to be able to work on Monday? These things must be prayed about individually; "I *am* thy servant; give me understanding, that I may know thy testimonies" (Psalm 119:125). At all times, though, it is the *spirit* of the commandment we need to honor, even though following the *letter* of it may become clouded.

Jesus made some allowances that we can use as guidelines. He worked on the Sabbath by healing infirmities, and then railed against some of the extremely literal interpretations of Scripture by the Pharisees who complained that He was violating the Sabbath by doing any work at all. He responded that it was okay to do good work on the Sabbath. (How many people work for their churches each Sunday as ministers, deacons, ushers, or parking attendants? The Lord will not hold it against them, but will instead magnify them for it.)

In addressing emergency situations, Jesus then asked them "Which of you shall have an ass or an ox fallen into a pit, and will not straightway pull him out on the sabbath day?" (Luke 14:5). His point is that we need to distinguish between lawful work and unlawful indulgences. "And he said unto them, The sabbath was made for man, and not man for the Sabbath" (Mark 2:27). It is a gift to us from God, intended for our welfare. Let each one of us determine, then, if we are acknowledging the endowment of that Sabbath gift through worship and thanksgiving, or are simply gratifying ourselves in our free time while ignoring God's blessings.

Many businesses are open on the Christian Sabbath day (Sunday), as well as on the Jewish Sabbath (Saturday). Employees are thereby required to work on those days or risk losing their jobs. In a faltering economy, when good jobs are scarce, many Christians are not inclined to gamble on their livelihood by refusing to work on Sundays. Thankfully, there are actions that can be taken to offset that commandment violation. Though some people may work on a Sunday, they can still attend religious services either before or after work. Bible study can also be maintained during the free hours of the day—before, during, or after work. We are to set aside the Sabbath as a day of devotion to the Lord, and reaf-

Politics

firm our faith and offer thanks. If we need to do so while squeezing in hours of employment, then we are still honoring the spirit of the law if we make special efforts to exalt God by remembering the sacredness of this holy day He has given us.

There are many individuals, however, who do not work on the Sabbath, yet still violate it. They may take a day of rest to fulfill the letter of the law, yet dishonor the spirit of it by neglecting God throughout the day. Instead, for them it becomes a day of sports events—usually accompanied with drinking—or a day of gambling spent at the track or the local casino. Some choose to sleep through the day (usually after a hard night's partying). Some choose to read all day, though without ever opening a Bible or biblical exposition. They do not attend worship services of any kind—even those freely available on television. Instead, they ignore God and all the loving kindnesses and special mercies He's bestowed upon them during the week, by refusing to establish a special communion with Him on this holy day and by giving Him thanks and praise.

And then there are those who openly mock followers of the fourth commandment, of whom some have been classified as bitter people clinging to religion. Others attack business owners for their Christian beliefs and for closing on Sundays to honor the Sabbath. Chick-fil-A, a fast-food chain, is one such business. The owners are devout Christians. They are closed on Thanksgiving, Christmas, and on Sundays. Because of their devotion to honoring God, they are viewed by secularists as dangerous radicals. For example, when Chick-fil-A opened a new store in Manhattan, an article appeared in The New Yorker magazine with the title *Chick-fil-A's Creepy Infiltration of New York City*, voicing the fear that "the brand's arrival here feels like an infiltration, in no small part because of its pervasive Christian traditionalism."[62] That "traditionalism" includes defending the biblical definition of marriage as only between a man and a woman. For that, they are branded as dangerous hate-mongers. When Twitter CEO Jack Dorsey tweeted (in June 2018) that he had ordered food

---

62 Piepenbring, Dan. "Chick-fil-A's Creepy Infiltration of New York City." The New Yorker. April 14, 2018. Accessed July 10, 2018. https://www.newyorker.com/culture/annals-of-gastronomy/chick-fil-as-creepy-infiltration-of-new-york-city?mbid=social_twitter.

from a Chick-fil-A restaurant, there was a social media outcry from the gay-rights crowd. He was forced to apologize first, and then promise never to eat another one of their (tasty) chicken sandwiches again, in order to obtain absolution for his "sin."

Boycotts have been organized against Chick-fil-A for their religious views by those generally affiliated with one political party. Those boycotts have backfired through political backlash from society and members of the other party. After the call for a boycott in 2012, for example, "The chain experienced what a spokesman called a 'record-setting day' on Wednesday as supporters thronged to many of its 1,600 locations, causing traffic jams and hours-long waits."[63] Which side of that political debate are you on? Are you hungry to defend Christian principles, or do you fast against defending the attack on them?

"HONOUR THY FATHER AND THY MOTHER: that thy days may be long upon the land which the LORD thy God giveth thee" (Exodus 20:12). This fifth commandment seems pretty straightforward. Children are to accept and yield to parental authority just as their parents accept God's authority over them; and respect of that relationship is to be continued throughout life. There is an established hierarchy which needs to be recognized and honored. Therefore, disobedience to the higher authority often requires disciplining through punishment in order to be corrected. Just as God chastises His people—"My son, do not make light of the Lord's discipline, and do not lose heart when he rebukes you, because the Lord disciplines the one he loves, and he chastens everyone he accepts as his son" (Hebrews 12:5–6, NIV)—so we are to discipline our children out of love as well to keep them from going astray. "The branch is easily bent when it is tender."[64] Do not allow it to become crooked, wayward, and hardened through a lack of early correction.

We will now explore how various facets of this commandment play out in the political arena.

The Bible states "He that spareth his rod hateth his son: but he

---

63 Cato, Jason, and Thomas Olson. "Chick-fil-A Boycott Backfire Not Surprising." TribLIVE.com. August 03, 2012. Accessed July 10, 2018. https://triblive.com/home/2329177-74/boycott-chick-fil-company-boycotts-cathy-consumer-foods-president-south.

64 Henry, *Commentary*, Vol. 3, 710.

that loveth him chasteneth him betimes" (Proverbs 13:24). The rod, commonly called a "switch" today, is usually a small, flexible tree branch stripped of its leaves, (though the term can also be applied towards hand-spanking). Its use is intended to inflict a temporary stinging rebuke to disobedience with the eye always towards correction. It should be noted that it does *not ever* give license to injure. Yet, there are many who feel that the parent has no right to discipline a child in such a manner, and so they seek to pass laws which redefine that accepted biblical practice as "child abuse." Generally, these same people are also advocates of the children's rights movement which usurps parental authority by giving children the same legal rights as their parents to make decisions over matters far beyond their limited, immature comprehension. This has led to legislation allowing children to obtain contraceptives or get abortions without parental consent.

To enforce this view, the government is enlisted as surrogate parent to protect the children *from their own parents*, as new wards of the state, often resulting in the children being turned away from them, as we saw happen in Nazi Germany with the Hitler Youth movement. Furthermore, government gets to decide the educational agenda for the child which oftentimes conflicts with parental religious beliefs. Russian revolutionary, Vladimir Lenin (1870-1924), once stated "Give me four years to teach the children and the seed I have sown will never be uprooted."[65] This leads to political indoctrination at the very earliest ages meant to offset biblical values imparted by the parents under the admonition to "Train up a child in the way he should go: and when he is old, he will not depart from it" (Proverbs 22:6). This educational usurpation—both religious and academic—has led to a great increase in homeschooling by parents wishing to retain authority over their child's upbringing. It is no wonder, then, that homeschooling is often under assault by secular governmental activists who feel *they* know best in how to raise *your* child.

Many universities foster a culture of defiance and rejection of traditional authority (parental or otherwise) under the guise of free speech and critical thinking. In the 1960s, that type of political activism adopted the slogan "Never trust anyone over

---

65 https://www.brainyquote.com/quotes/vladimir_lenin_153238

thirty"—in direct opposition to biblical teaching which demands "Likewise, ye younger, submit yourselves unto the elder. Yea, all *of you* be subject one to another, and be clothed with humility: for God resisteth the proud, and giveth grace to the humble" (1 Peter 5:5). Rather than "Hear counsel, and receive instruction, that thou mayest be wise in thy latter end" (Proverbs 19:20), they've been taught to reject the accepted wisdom of the ages so that "[p]rofessing themselves to be wise, they became fools" (Romans 1:22). Ironically, those seeds of the *free speech* rebellion, which challenged established wisdom, have germinated into total *speech censorship* on campuses of any views they disagree with. A new report from higher-education watchdog group Campus Reform highlights the extreme disparity of speakers from one particular political party over the other in ratios of 44-4 (University of Indiana); 64-2 (SUNY-Albany); 30-9 (George Washington University); 9-2 (Alabama); 44-2 (Vermont).[66] Those proposing a differing political ideology—deemed politically incorrect—are either declined an invitation or, if ever allowed to speak, are shouted down, threatened with violence, or run off campus—despite their status as elders. So much for the free exchange of ideas universities were originally designed for. They have now become institutions of mindless totalitarian indoctrination.

    Another way in which politics has intruded upon this commandment is in the treatment of parents when they become elderly. Children who were taught to reject tradition through today's revolutionary politics often become young adults who assume an air of arrogant superiority over their aging parents and thereby dishonor them. Condescension and impatience are warning signs of a growing disrespect. When geriatric parents begin to require special hands-on treatment, many children who have grown up in this age of me-first selfishness are reluctant to provide it—forgetting how they were cared for in their helplessness as infants and children by their parents. Instead, easy methods are sought to alleviate the increasing demand of caring for the elderly. Many seniors are quickly shipped off to nursing

---

66 Board, Post Editorial. "When Colleges Say 'inclusive,' What They Really Mean Is No Conservatives." New York Post. July 23, 2018. Accessed July 23, 2018. https://nypost.com/2018/07/22/when-colleges-say-inclusive-what-they-really-mean-is-no-conservatives/.

homes and are all but forgotten by their ungrateful children who willingly abrogated their responsibility to reciprocal care during their parents' time of increasing helplessness, thereby dishonoring the commandment.

And then, there are those who advocate for a quick termination of all suffering—both of their parents' in illness or infirmity, and of their own as reluctant caregivers. Euthanasia, also known as "mercy killing" or "assisted suicide," is murder, plain and simple. It usurps God's absolute authority over life and death. Hebrews 9:27 states that "... it is appointed unto men once to die ...." That appointment is by the decree of God alone. It may seem noble to alleviate the suffering that comes with disease, illness, and old age, but it defies God's will that we bear any thorn in the flesh He appoints us to bear. His design for afflictions is to purge out corruptions in our souls and prepare us for heaven. They are meant for our good. "Is any among you afflicted? let him pray" (James 5:13). When Paul appealed to God to remove the plaguing thorn from his side (whatever it was: illness, infirmity, opposition to the gospel, etc.), he received his answer: "And he said unto me, My grace is sufficient for thee: for my strength is made perfect in weakness" (2 Corinthians 12:9). Had Paul defiantly rejected that humbling thorn in his side and thrown off his work, we would not have his many epistles, nor his evangelizing, which have brought many billions to Christ.

Afflictions are sent to bring us closer to God by awakening conscience and bringing sin to remembrance; "For thou writest bitter things against me, and makest me to possess the iniquities of my youth" (Job 13:26). They are sent, not to devastate us, but to bring us to spiritual maturity by having us rely more and more upon His strength in our weakness. "Before I was afflicted I went astray: but now have I kept thy word" (Psalm 119:67). What if healthy people dead to religion all their life (and therefore slated for an eternity in hell cut off from God forever) were suddenly diagnosed with a deadly disease? Facing imminent mortality, they might wisely seek to find out what awaits them after death, and earnestly enquire into religion. This in turn, might bring them to repentance and forgiveness through Christ, thereby assuring them heavenly bliss in eternity instead of perpetual torment. Committing suicide, however, to avoid the suffering from that disease, precludes any hope of that spiritual salvation. They would die in their sins and pay for them forever. Therefore, avoiding that affliction of suffering is rejecting God's hidden grace meant to bring us to repentance—before we die and the sentence of hell is irrevocably fixed.

As for the faithful, we are all God's servants in this world. We cannot quit His service because the road suddenly becomes rough. "When times are good, be happy; but when times are bad, consider this: God has made the one as well as the other. Therefore, no one can discover anything about their future" (Ecclesiastes 7:14, NIV). Whatever road is laid before us, we must travel it. Whatever burdens are laid upon us, we must bear them. Job endured some of the greatest afflictions imaginable under Satan's direction. Yet, though he lamented his birth, he never considered suicide. As Matthew Henry noted "However uneasy soever the soul's confinement in the body may be, it must by no means break prison, but wait for a fair discharge."[67] It is not our call to make. We must at all times remember that the body is the temple of the soul, and that defiling that body through suicide destroys the temple wherein dwells the Lord through the Holy Spirit. "Know ye not that ye are the temple of God, and *that* the Spirit of God dwelleth in you? If any man defile the temple of God, him shall God destroy; for the temple of God is holy, which *temple* ye are. Let no man deceive himself. If any man among you seemeth to be wise in this world, let him become a fool, that he may be wise" (1 Corinthians 3:16-18). The seeming wisdom of this world to end suffering through suicide trusts the lies of Satan, whose only goal for you is to ensure suffering for eternity in the next—sharing in his punishment.

So, do your personal politics permit the choice on whether or not to use corporal punishment in disciplining unruly children according to biblical guidelines? Do you believe that parents are better equipped to love and raise children within the nuclear family setting than an indifferent government would be in raising them as wards of the state? Do you believe that through teaching stable religious principles, parents can instill

---

67 Henry, *Commentary*, Vol. 3, 31.

Politics

better values in children than the ever-shifting politically correct indoctrination of the public school systems?

Do you believe that parental respect is a lifelong commitment and not limited to the years of childhood through adolescence? Do you believe in the personal duty of rendering care to elderly parents (absent the need for hospitalization or professional nursing management) as they become increasingly feeble in their senior years? Do you believe that suicide is self-murder and that assisting suicide makes you equally complicit in that crime? Can you see how the first steps on the slippery slope of assisted suicide to alleviate *physical suffering* have now led to promoting euthanasia for all manner of dissatisfaction in life—even *personal boredom*?[68]

Once again, you must decide if the political party you support is in alignment with God's will regarding this fifth commandment (as discussed in part above) or not. If not, then your politics have become blasted by Satan and you are being deceived into thinking that your regressive views are somehow progressive.

THE MORAL IMPERATIVE OF THE SIXTH COMMANDMENT, "Thou shalt not kill," is not as straightforward as many people may think. Didn't God command that certain sins required death as punishment? In fact, it was God who established capital punishment for murderers in Genesis 9:6: "Whoso sheddeth man's blood, by man shall his blood be shed." Didn't He also command the generals of Israel to kill their enemies during wartime? Didn't the priests of Israel kill animals for sacrifice as prescribed by God? Don't even vegans kill plants for food? Obviously, there are exceptions to a blanket condemnation of any form of killing.

The Hebrew verb *ratsakh* is better translated as *murder* than as *kill*. Therefore, a more accurate translation of the commandment is "Thou shalt not murder." Because murder is generally defined as the *unlawful* killing of human life without justification or excuse, many seem to think that abortion is therefore *not*

---

68 O'Brien, Zoie. "Bored to Death: ASSISTED SUICIDE to Be Granted for People Who Are Simply Fed-up of Living." Express.co.uk. October 13, 2016. Accessed July 17, 2018. https://www.express.co.uk/news/world/720883/Euthanasia-granted-Holland-completed-life-Dutch-Suicide.

murder because it has as recently as 1973 become legal in the United States through the judicial fiat of seven unelected judges on a politically stacked Supreme Court—despite the majority of people being against unrestricted abortion, as all polls consistently show. Because judicial activism has been the primary method used by one political party to advance unpopular positions (thereby circumventing the will of the people as expressed at the ballot box), we've seen hysteria in this country by some, over the recent vacancy of a Supreme Court seat. Their fears were that the position would be filled with a Constitutional constructionist—one who simply *interprets* the law as a judge, rather than *writing* law as a legislator. A solid 5-4 majority of originalists (versus activists) on the court after the 2018 appointment could tip the balance away from the Roe v Wade social legislation mindset, in favor of ruling on laws based upon the Constitution. Even then, should that misguided ruling ever be overturned (however unlikely), it would simply send the abortion issue back to the 50 states to be decided individually. Yet advocates know that some states will make the practice illegal. Their concern is that it may eventually become a national trend, hence their abject horror at the thought—as witnessed by the extreme apocalyptic hyperbole being employed against any proposed judicial nominees by the current President who favors originalists on the court.

Predating these justices by thousands of years, however, the early Christian church has always condemned abortion. The *Didache*—also known as *The Teaching of the Twelve Apostles*—is a first-century Christian treatise. It states in 2.2 that "thou shalt not procure abortion, nor commit infanticide."[69] The reason for this is clearly stated by God: "Before I formed thee in the belly I knew thee; and before thou camest forth out of the womb I sanctified thee" (Jeremiah 1:5); also, "I was cast upon thee from the womb: thou *art* my God from my mother's belly" (Psalm 22:10). God sees our lives in totality and plans them for us even before conception.

Human life, therefore, begins at conception. Upon fertilization of the egg by the sperm, the resulting zygote is human life

---

69 CO Now LLC. ~The Didache~ II, 2. Accessed July 17, 2018. http://www.thedidache.com/.

in its earliest stage. It contains a full genetic complement which, if nurtured, will progress through all the stages of human life from embryo to adult. Because it is only a small mass of cells in the early stages of development, many people claim it is not yet a person and therefore disposable. The debate over abortion as murder, then, is really a debate over whether human life at any stage is sacred and should be protected, or if human life only attains legal rights upon personhood—which then needs two questions to be asked: What defines personhood? Who makes that decision? Conveniently ignored is that God has already determined the answers to those questions when He told Jeremiah that even while he was in the womb, "I ordained thee a prophet unto the nations" (Jeremiah 1:5). God pre-ordains a purpose for every embryo conceived, thereby conferring personhood upon each while yet in the womb. To correct PETA's Ingrid Newkirk, A fetus is an infant; is a toddler; is a schoolchild; is a teenager; is a young adult; is a middle-aged person; is a senior citizen. There is no one stage of development more important than another to God. He sees us in our totality.

Not content with first trimester abortions—justified as simply removing a "clump of cells"—the pro-abortion lobby has constantly pushed for abortion on demand at any stage. As a result, we now witness the grisly acts of partial-birth abortion committed on fully-developed babies while in the womb—pre-birth canal—whose tiny bodies are then removed and discarded as aborted "fetuses" despite their full development as infants. This is nothing short of infanticide. In a dramatic escalation of the war on fetuses, the New York State Senate passed a pro-abortion bill on January 22, 2019, which Governor Andrew Cuomo signed into law.

> That law codified abortion in the state constitution, legalized abortions up until the moment of birth, allowed any "medical practitioner" to perform abortions, denied "personhood" to babies until after they were born and removed the requirement to aid a baby that survived an abortion and all references to abortion from the criminal penal codes, among other despicable things. After the

bill was signed into law, New York Democrats led a celebratory standing ovation in the legislative chamber.[70]

Consider the spiritual retribution by God against people cheering a law which allows for babies to be killed on their due dates during the mother's labor—even by non-doctors; and if the baby survived that assassination attempt, is still allowed to be murdered on the table afterwards without any legal prosecution for the murderer!

> Karen Korakis writes to the NY Post: "Aside from being completely appalled and sickened by the flagrant disregard for human life, I must point out that a late-term abortion into the third trimester would have to be considered a violent death. As such, the cause and manner of death would have to be certified by a medical examiner or coroner. ... As a former New York City medical examiner under the late Dr. Charles S. Hirsch, I wonder how the manner of death at the hand of another would be certified. In my professional opinion, homicide would be the only appropriate choice."[71]

Abortion advocates claim that protecting the mother's life was more important than protecting the baby's life, and so we were told initially that abortions were rare, and performed for the most part to save the life of the mother. That turned out to be a great lie. Most abortions performed have nothing whatsoever to do with preserving the mother's health but are instead performed because the pregnancy is deemed inconvenient. As for abortions being rare, since the Roe v Wade ruling in 1973 making abortion legal in all fifty states, there have been over 60 million babies aborted in America. That total exceeds the total number

---

70 Marquis, Ben. "Rush Limbaugh on NY Abortion Law: 'Here's Why Liberals Are Cheering Murder.'" *The Western Journal*, The Wildcard, 30 Jan. 2019, accessed February 02, 2019. www.westernjournal.com/ct/rush-limbaugh-ny-abortion-law-liberals-cheering-murder/.

71 Goodwin, Michael. "License to Kill." New York Post. February 03, 2019. Accessed February 03, 2019. https://nypost.com/2019/02/02/democrats-are-leaving-hillary-clinton-behind/.

of people killed in World War I (40 million), and is comparable to the death toll of WWII, (50–80 million). Clearly, we have waged a brutal war on the unborn. Author David Kupelian notes "More than 3,000 innocent babies [are] slain in their mothers' wombs every single day (the same number as died in the Sept. 11, 2001, terror attacks)."[72] Advocates also claim that a woman has a right to control her own body. That is true for *her* body, but it does not include the additional body of the baby within her, entrusted to her care by God, with expected outside care from the father—whose baby it also is.

The opposing sides of the debate basically represent a pro-life versus a pro-death attitude regarding the unborn. No wonder, then, that advocates for abortion must couch their extreme positions in euphemisms or risk total rejection by the public. Use of the positive term *pro-choice* is therefore necessary to mask the negative implications of *pro-abortion*. Despite the circumlocution around the abortion word, nevertheless, they are willfully *choosing* to terminate an innocent human life. The political divide in this nation over that singular issue is quite stark.

Paradoxically, those who favor the right to terminate an innocent life almost always happen to abhor the idea of those who are guilty of homicide being put to death through capital punishment. Not only that, many of them advocate further for the *release* of convicted murderers—as we've seen recently happen here in New York City with the parole of two men—one of whom slaughtered two police officers after first luring them into an ambush with a phony call of distress.

The death penalty for murder and other acts of depraved indifference is sanctioned by God in the Old Testament, as noted above (Genesis 9:6), and ratified in the New Testament as well. "For rulers are not a terror to good works, but to the evil. Wilt thou then not be afraid of the power? ... For he is the minister of God to thee for good. But if thou do that which is evil, be afraid; for he beareth not the sword in vain: for he is the minister of God, a revenger to *execute* wrath upon him that doeth evil" (Romans 13:3–4). Courtroom justice served upon murderers avenges the

---

72 Kupelian, David, WND, and Facebook. "How the Left Revels in Violating the 10 Commandments." WND. Accessed July 26, 2018. https://www.wnd.com/2016/03/how-the-left-revels-in-violating-the-10-commandments/.

victims, whose spilled blood cries out to God from the ground for the wrong to be made right, (see Genesis 4:10). It gives the victims' families a measure of closure as well. Pleading for mercy, therefore, by those who were not the injured party or affected at all by the crime, is not at all as noble as they might project. Most times, it is the result of misguided people joining an unjust cause. Their virtue-signaling marches and prison protests are an affront to God, the family, and justice, because they ignore the suffering of those immediately affected and they diminish the value of the life taken by denying justice. "For every man shall bear his own burden" (Galatians 6:5). It is especially hypocritical in those who support taking innocent lives through abortion.

The two diametrically opposed viewpoints of being pro-abortion and anti-capital punishment have become major political issues in which the political parties have fallen one way or the other. For whom do cast your vote? Does it comport with the will of God?

And then there is a form of symbolic murder known as character assassination. This is what is known most commonly as the politics of personal destruction. Disagree with a certain political ideology and suddenly you are portrayed as bigoted, and hateful. Disagree with abortion on demand and you are a sexist. Disagree with redefining marriage as between a man and a woman, and you are homophobic. Desiring to see the national borders secured against the massive influx of illegal aliens somehow makes you a racist. Agreeing with a ban on the free entry of people into this country from a few terror-sponsoring nations, and you are vilified as Islamophobic. Many lives and careers have been destroyed by these untruthful appellations. Many honorable reputations have been murdered simply because of a personal perspective in opposition to the so-called politically correct views, as determined solely by the opposing party. (This issue will be discussed further under the ninth commandment—dealing with the matter of bearing false witness.)

THE SEVENTH COMMANDMENT, "Thou shalt not commit adultery" (Exodus 20:14), is twofold in meaning. Taken literally, it is about fidelity between husband and wife. "Marriage *is* honourable in

Politics

all, and the bed undefiled: but whoremongers and adulterers God will judge" (Hebrews 13:4). Taken symbolically, it is about fidelity between humanity and God; "And I saw, when for all the causes whereby backsliding Israel committed adultery I had put her away, and given her a bill of divorce; yet her treacherous sister Judah feared not, but went and played the harlot also" (Jeremiah 3:8). God often used the term adultery to decry Israel's unfaithfulness through idolatry.

It is generally accepted that those who consider themselves religious in any way have a much lower susceptibility towards adultery than do those without religion, simply because there is a measure of devotion involved. If they do succumb to it, they certainly don't condone it, since they suffer guilt because of it. That guilt eventually forces many away from the illicit relationship in repentance.

Those without religion, on the other hand, are much bolder and have even written articles arguing for the morality of adultery, stating that, with two consenting adults, the act is victimless. Anyone who objects to it is merely imposing his or her own morality upon others, and because adopting religion is a matter of choice (which the engagers have rejected), any pain inflicted upon the injured spouse is the self-inflicted result of misbegotten religious expectations.

Unfortunately, because adultery is a sin of the flesh, we, as humans, are all subject to its temptation. The result is that people of all occupations, persuasions, religions, and politics have succumbed to it. The gravest sin of Israel's King David (a man after God's own heart even) was committing adultery with Bathsheba and then trying to cover up her pregnancy by sending her husband, Uriah, to the front lines to be killed so that he wouldn't discover her unfaithfulness.

There is no political party in the United States that openly advocates for adultery—not yet, anyway. This shows that most are in agreement over its sin nature and that publicly supporting it is not politically expedient. However, those secretly sympathetic to it can be discovered. They are generally the same people who wage war on religious expression, have reworked the definition of marriage, and advocate for open marriages. They believe in easy, no-fault divorce. Their politics are sympathetic to the communists, socialists, and fascists who believe in replacing the family with government. What better way to achieve that goal than fostering divorce through infidelity? These issues have been explored previously in this work (Chapter Twelve) and will not be expanded upon much further here. It should be noted, though, that many of the "free love" radicals of the 1960s countercultural movement have now taken up seats of power in the government. Supporting them at the ballot box advances their countercultural sympathies to defy this commandment.

In the United States, there exists a representative government of the people, by the people, and for the people. Elected officials are obligated to voice the will of the people who elected them, and vote accordingly to promote it. Political infidelity occurs when politicians vow one thing on the campaign trail just to get elected, such as *cutting* taxes, but then vote against those promises, by *raising* taxes once in office. This is political adultery. Beware the flattering lip service of self-serving politicians who say one thing but do the opposite. Check their voting records to see how they voted over any issue that had religious implications such as same-sex marriage, Israel, morality, etc. If they vote consistently against the Bible's teachings on these issues, then vote against them in the next election, regardless of political affiliation. Otherwise, you are aiding and abetting the enemy in his campaign of social, moral, and religious decline.

"THOU SHALT NOT STEAL" (Exodus 20:15). This eighth commandment has a very broad application throughout society. Just because one may never have engaged in shoplifting does not necessarily mean such a person has not violated this commandment. As discussed in Business and Industry (Chapter Thirteen), taking home office supplies, showing up late for work, taking extended breaks and meals, using social media on company time, etc., are all forms of stealing. Other forms of stealing include taking credit for another's accomplishments. That is reputation-stealing. Claiming to have served in a war zone, as many military veteran politicians have done who yet never left stateside while in the service, is stolen valor. Cheating on exams to pass the class is academic theft. Plagiarism is intellectual theft, etc.

Politics has its own version of stealing which is especially devious because politicians do it legally. They've designed an unfair progressive tax code that actually punishes achievement. The Bible established the law of tithing—paying 10 percent of the first fruits (total gross income before taxation). Today, we have seven different tax brackets ranging from 10 percent to 37 percent, depending upon household income. Yet, almost half (43.9 percent) of American households pay no taxes at all to the federal government. In fact, they *receive* money from the government while the top 20 percent pay almost 90 percent of all taxes.

How is this fair? Why do the people accept this? Because they are told by politicians that those who earn more are greedy and need to pay their "fair share." Never mind that they are unfairly paying the lion's share already! Sowing class-warfare envy has become the chosen weapon of politicians to facilitate stealing from the more productive members of society by promoting the misleading idea that the poor are poor because the rich are rich. But it's not a zero-sum game. One person's gain does not mean another person's loss. Profiting from hard work and due diligence does not create the poverty resulting from drug addiction, single-parent households, and willful unemployment through laziness.

Unfortunately, personal application of one's talents and abilities, as well as taking financial risk through exposure, are penalized with confiscation and redistribution—as if punishing the rich will somehow uplift the poor. In the end, it's all a massive vote-buying scheme by those *pretending* to care for the poor. Rob Peter to pay Paul and you'll always have Paul's vote—that is, until the system collapses through Peter's forced bankruptcy. Former British Prime Minister, Margaret Thatcher (1925–2013), noted that "[t]he trouble with socialism is that eventually you run out of other people's money." Have you succumbed to the political allure of "free stuff" and are living off the fruits of someone else's labor? Then you need only look to the economic disaster in Venezuela to see the results of protracted Socialism, where zoo animals are being slaughtered just to feed the people.

If you support this unfair taxation practice through your political choices, you need to reassess your values and get them in line with biblical principles. If, instead of emulating the work ethics required to achieve wealth you begrudge the legitimately earned wealth and prosperity of others, then you have been manipulated by Satan into feeling an unjustified bitterness and resentment. Does your political party foster that type of resentment to garner votes, under the promise that wealth redistribution will correct income inequality? If so, you need to redistribute your votes away from them.

THE NINTH COMMANDMENT states "Thou shalt not bear false witness against thy neighbour" (Exodus 20:16). Though this applies on an interpersonal level through malice, revenge, or an attempt at profit, it is often employed in politics through character assassination and deliberately deceitful campaigns of propaganda. These techniques of propaganda are worth investigating to help uncover the truth of matters.

Character assassination is achieved through *ad hominem* attacks on a person's character to avoid addressing the political issues. They involve misportrayal of a political view as being racist, sexist, etc. *Appeals to fear* (fearmongering) are made by politicians in attempts to persuade the electorate that if the opponent wins the election, people will starve and die, and the world as we know it will basically end. We see *bandwagon* propaganda employed whenever you hear about a consensus of people agreeing to a certain political point of view—such as science being "settled" because a consensus of scientists agree when, in fact, there is no real consensus. It is simply an attempt to persuade the target audience to join the manufactured majority.

Perhaps the most devious propaganda campaigns come from the mainstream media, who come as wolves in sheep's clothing under the guise of objectivity and fairness. Their *agenda setting* techniques include force-feeding certain social issues and news items onto the public which promote their politics, while omitting to report on news unfavorable to their causes. The allegedly "free press" in this nation has become nothing less than a Ministry of Propaganda promoting one political party's agenda. They attack the opposition relentlessly while providing cover for the failures, malfeasance, and criminality of their own party members. They apply a false narrative to a political situation to create *the big lie* which they then repeat endlessly as accepted fact. They promote campaigns of disinformation through false testimony or documentation which they also report as fact—and if caught (as with Journalist Dan Rather's 2004 "Memogate" scandal), justify it as being "fake but accurate" nonetheless. Fortunately, they are finally being called out on all their biases. As a result, 77 percent of people recently polled believe that major news outlets report "fake news."[73]

THE TENTH COMMANDMENT warns against wrongful desires: "Thou shalt not covet thy neighbour's house, thou shalt not covet thy neighbour's wife, nor his manservant, nor his maidservant, nor his ox, nor his ass, nor any thing that *is* thy neighbour's" (Exodus 20:17). Replacing God in the heart with a yearning for anything else is the major sin referenced by this commandment because covetousness is idolatry, (see Colossians 3:5).

Today in America, we no longer have servants (slaves). Hi-tech machinery has replaced the labor of oxen and asses in the fields (except in certain "Plain People" communities such as the Amish). In their places, we have come to covet other possessions of our neighbors, such as expensive homes, cars, jewelry, clothing, prestige, wealth, technology, etc. Coveting "thy neighbor's wife" has already been discussed under the commandment forbidding adultery, so coveting thy neighbor's *goods* will be the chief focus here.

Coveting is the immoral and selfish desire for that which is not ours. Attempting to obtain illicit interests can lead to theft, adultery, murder, and even war because it elevates material desires over spiritual fulfillment. Jesus warned us against materialism; "Lay not up for yourselves treasures upon earth, where moth and rust doth corrupt, and where thieves break through and steal: But lay up for yourselves treasures in heaven, where neither moth nor rust doth corrupt, and where thieves do not

---

73 Blanc, Jarrett, Edward-Isaac Dovere, Gordon F. Sander, Alireza Nader, and CRISTIANO LIMA. "Poll: 77 Percent Say Major News Outlets Report 'fake News'." About Us. April 02, 2018. Accessed July 24, 2018. https://www.politico.com/story/2018/04/02/poll-fake-news-494421.

break through nor steal: For where your treasure is, there will your heart be also" (Matthew 6:19–21). Introspection into what really occupies our hearts is required to unmask any covetousness hidden within our souls.

In politics, covetousness is also known as envy. It is no wonder then that some politicians stoke that fire for political gain. Wealth-redistribution schemes *pretend* to correct that injustice—to garner votes from the aggrieved—but can never actually achieve equality due to the myriad other factors involved in attaining prosperity. Class-warfare tactics such as pitting the poor against the rich is a classic tried-and-true strategy of communism and socialism. The century-old Marxist political warfare instigated by the proletariat/bourgeoisie construct of old is revived today in the 99 percent versus the 1 percent *Occupy* movement which demands wealth redistribution as a form of reparation.

Winston Churchill correctly called socialism the "gospel of envy." Through envy, cold war is established between the "haves" and the "have-nots." Fostering envy ensures an unfulfilling, discontented life for the "have-nots" thereby overruling the wisdom of St. Paul who wrote, "Not that I speak in respect of want: for I have learned, in whatsoever state I am, *therewith* to be content" (Philippians 4:11). Contentment is anathema, therefore, to those who sow and exploit discontent for political gain.

Envy breeds anger and indignation through our focusing on the lives of others over our own. Those who succumb to it resent their neighbor's prosperity or success as if it was somehow attained at their expense. *Social justice warriors* weaponize that ideology by creating a grievance industry which promotes and exploits racism against so-called *white privilege,* and sexism against the so-called *patriarchy*; while creating new categories for disgruntled protest such as *cultural appropriation* and other various *microaggressions*—which then require the need for *safe spaces* and *trigger warnings* for those easily offended by differing viewpoints. These devices are all intended to promote disparity, discord, and intolerance for opposing views, while promoting the false ideology that the evils of this world can be corrected by those given enough governmental power to rule over the lives of others. Jesus Christ assured us that "Blessed *are* they which do hunger and thirst after righteousness: for they shall be filled" (Matthew 5:6). But this will only happen "[w]hen Christ, *who is our life, shall appear, then shall ye also appear with him in glory*" (Colossians 3:4). Injustice will always be with us until Christ's return, because no human is yet perfected. From Moses to Jesus, Bible wisdom has declared that "the poor shall never cease out of the land" (Deuteronomy 15:11). "For ye have the poor always with you" (Matthew 26:11). Those who promise to right all wrongs and end injustice and poverty forever are deceivers. They are flawed, imperfect human beings just like the rest of us. They do not deserve your vote of confidence in their solutions, or your vote for them at the ballot box if they promise to deliver heaven on earth. It is not within their power to do so and never will be. That transformative power resides within the purview of Heaven alone.

Scripture has provided for us a great guide to use in judging our personal politics, but what of the other hot-button political issues of the day, unaddressed directly by the Ten Commandments? Unfortunately, many of them fall under the category of biblical *abominations*. Paul's letter to the Romans reiterates the prohibitions of the Ten Commandments and mentions other things deplorable to God as well, (see Romans 1:24–32). Those sins listed are ever deplorable to a God who does not bend to our situational ethics. Hating the sin is not the same thing as hating the sinner. We are all sinners and need to love each other as brothers and sisters. But we must not promote sin (or the acceptance of it) at the ballot box because of a misguided compassion, or display spiritual cowardice because of fear in being seen as politically incorrect.

Political Correctness (as discussed previously in Chapter Three) is an authoritarian weapon used to bludgeon opponents of differing political viewpoints into silence. Its design is to conceal the truth. It is a favored weapon of the Communist Party. In fact, it has been said that PC originated with the CP. In America, more and more people have become fed up with other people dictating to us what we can and can't say or believe. According to a new poll, 71 percent of Americans "*believe that political correctness has silenced important discussions our society needs to have.*"⁷⁴ Succumbing to it shows political cowardice and is warned against in Scripture; "The fear of man bringeth a snare: but whoso putteth his trust in the LORD shall be safe" (Proverbs 29:25). Stand up for biblical principles and vote accordingly. Do not allow others to shame, isolate, or marginalize your religious beliefs either in private or in public. That's all part of the Saul Alinsky method, an American political activist (1909–1972) who wrote *Rules for Radicals*. His political strategy included "Pick the target, freeze it, personalize it, and polarize it," while offering that "Ridicule is man's most potent weapon." It's no wonder, then, that he dedicated his book to Lucifer.

The key to obeying the Ten Commandments is to:

> Owe no man any thing, but to love one another: for he that loveth another hath fulfilled the law. For this, Thou shalt not commit adultery, Thou shalt not kill, Thou shalt not steal, Thou shalt not bear false witness, Thou shalt not covet; and if *there be* any other commandment, it is briefly comprehended in this saying, namely, Thou shalt love thy neighbour as thyself. Love worketh no ill to his neighbour: therefore love *is* the fulfilling of the law (Romans 13:8–10).

Let your politics reflect the love of others—not by conforming to the ever-changing political correctness of the day in defiance of Scripture, but by retaining the permanence of Scripture in its promise for the eternal salvation of the soul.

---

[74] "Majority of Americans Want Right to Express Unpopular Opinions, Even If It Offends – Poll." RT International. Accessed July 28, 2018. https://www.rt.com/usa/408444-political-correctness-discussion-poll/.

16

Conclusion

It has been shown throughout Scripture, throughout history, and through the events in our own lives that there is indeed a spiritual war for our souls. All conflicts in life—personal, professional, national, and international—come from Satan. He is the root cause of all strife. His sole intention is for our destruction as he vies with God for our personal devotion through the promotion and acceptance of his rebellious ways. He is a general in search of recruits for his volunteer army of rebels. As such, he wages a lifelong war against God through temptation, lies, and deceit for the dominance of our eternal souls.

However, as he cannot *force* us to do anything against our will, his war amounts to a Cold War campaign of carnal propaganda intended to sow hostility against the spiritual and holy ways of God. His constant temptations can be an overwhelming force—like gravity—pulling many of the unwary ever-downward away from God towards hell. He is the animating force behind the entropy of the world. He erodes and decays all that is good. He transformed the perfect order of blissful peace in the Garden of Eden into the disordered state of the warring world today. His all-out terms of warfare against humanity are waged on a macro scale against nations as well as on a micro scale against individuals. Proof in his existence has been established. There is an enemy. Proof of his infernal mission has been confirmed. There is a very real threat playing out as a coup against God. It is up to each of us, then, to take up the spiritual arms available in order to quell his incitement to rebellion within our souls.

Scripture portrays military imagery through many examples of spiritual/physical battle-warfare similitude. This battle-guide book has expanded upon those military metaphorical exercises. Adopting a martial mindset against temptation to sin is necessary in preserving our spiritual fortifications. As individuals, we need to study the methods of soldiering in order to combat the attempted enemy infiltrations. We must continue to uphold the banner of God throughout our lives and never surrender it.

Along with any combat modeling we adopt to address daily assaults upon our values, faith, and spiritual fortitude, it is also necessary to develop a system of intelligence gathering and interpretation to discover ambushes, and to limit the first-strike capabilities of the enemy. Counterintelligence and threat awareness information will eliminate or minimize damage the enemy intends. Knowing in advance the specific personal weaknesses the adversary intends to exploit as targets will do much towards thwarting those specific aggressions. Therefore, knowing yourself is as imperative as knowing your enemy.

It also becomes necessary to detect enemy infiltration within our social and professional circles by unmasking propaganda campaigns. Spies come in all shapes and sizes. Many are willing advocates for Satan's policies even without consciously embracing them. They do not believe in God (or the devil for that matter), and so they live according to the flesh while advising others to do the same. Their philosophy is "let us eat and drink; for to morrow we die" (1 Corinthians 15:32). Other spies are misguided dupes (people Vladimir Lenin labeled as "useful idiots"), promoting specific evils under the guise of a concerned compassion. And sometimes, even the faithful can become temporarily confused and deceived into aiding and abetting the enemy's plan—as we saw with Peter rebuking Jesus about going to Jerusalem to die for us and redeem humanity—see Matthew 16:21-23.

New-age philosophies, self-help guides, personal empowerment, positive thinking, transcendental meditation—these are all distractions if they don't accept Jesus Christ as the one true path to peace and spiritual freedom. We are warned against them in Scripture; "Now the Spirit speaketh expressly, that in the latter times some shall depart from the faith, giving heed to seducing

Conclusion

spirits, and doctrines of devils" (1 Timothy 4:1). The world seems intent on embracing everything *but* Jesus Christ as the way to salvation.

Politics has become the new battleground in the war for the soul. The extreme polarization we are currently witnessing is resulting in violence and even attempted murder. Political Correctness—as determined by one political party—results in the adoption of a right-versus-wrong mentality, allowing for no margin of deviation. People are assaulted regularly for wearing the wrong political hat. People are shot playing baseball for being a member of the wrong political party. Offices of political opponents experience bricks thrown through their windows or suffer incidents of arson. Family members are harassed at home and at restaurants for their association with members of the wrong presidential administration. Opposing viewpoints are shouted down and guest speakers are met with violence on campuses across America. Vandalism of homes and property occur for posting an incorrect lawn sign. Automobiles are vandalized for posting the wrong political bumper stickers. People are refused service at certain establishments because of their political affiliations. Others are targeted for lawsuits because of their incorrect beliefs. Riots to "resist" the wrong existing political order have become commonplace. Death threats are now a predominant feature in the lives of those supporting the wrong political causes or candidates. The list of fascist, violent incidents against political opposition members and groups grows on an almost daily basis.[75] The country is slowly being driven to civil war—and all the while Satan smiles approvingly.

Biblical prophecy warns us of these times. "Then shall they deliver you up to be afflicted, and shall kill you: and ye shall be hated of all nations for my name's sake. And then shall many be offended, and shall betray one another, and shall hate one another. And many false prophets shall rise, and shall deceive many. And because iniquity shall abound, the love of many shall wax cold" (Matthew 24:9–12). Hate is certainly ruling the day.

---

75 Nolte, John. "Rap Sheet: ***555** Acts of Media-Approved Violence and Harassment Against Trump Supporters." Breitbart. August 17, 2018. Accessed August 30, 2018. https://www.breitbart.com/big-journalism/2018/07/05/rap-sheet-acts-of-media-approved-violence-and-harassment-against-trump-supporters/.

The United States of America was founded as a "Nation under God." Yet politics have fractured the country into opposing camps of saints versus heretics. Half the country now openly advocates for biblical abominations expressly forbidden by God in Scripture. Surely, the end times are upon us. "O *ye* hypocrites, ye can discern the face of the sky; but can ye not *discern* the signs of the times?" (Matthew 16:3). Biblical prophecies predicting the end times have all been realized. There is nothing left unfulfilled in prophetic Scripture to deter or delay the triumphant return of Jesus Christ. It may happen now in the twinkling of an eye. "Watch therefore, for ye know neither the day nor the hour wherein the Son of man cometh" (Matthew 25:13). Therefore, we must be girded for battle at every moment, and fight the long fight, so that when our Supreme Commander, the Lord Jesus Christ, returns to lead us in the final battle of Armageddon against the forces of evil, we are found to be willing conscripts into His victorious army. May God bless and strengthen you for that glorious day.

About the Author

Dave G. Becher was born in Queens, NY, and raised on Long Island. He attained a B.A. from Stonybrook University. He has been reading and studying the Bible for over twenty-five years. This is his third published work. The two previously published books include a categorized compilation of Matthew Henry quotes *Applying the Wisdom of the Word* and a three-part theological treatise on the omniscience, omnipotence, and mercies of God, *The Tripartite Helmet of Hope and Salvation*.

Also by Dave G. Becher

Applying the Wisdom of the Word

The wisdom of English minister Matthew Henry (1662-1714) has been gleaned from his masterwork *Commentary On The Whole Bible* and organized under two general headings—Wisdom and Folly—representing the basic dos and don'ts for the eternal soul. Each general heading is then sub-divided into multiple chapter headings dealing with topics relevant to everyday life.

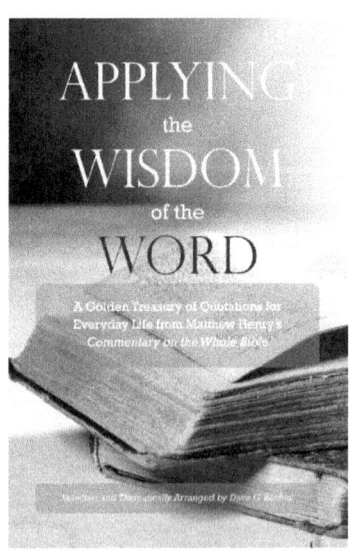

Also by Dave G. Becher

The Tripartite Helmet of Hope and Salvation

Part one of this work thoroughly documents the many instances of Biblical prophecy fulfilled within Scripture as well as in history outside of the Bible. Part two contains discourses on the many miracles in Scripture in both the Old and New Testaments, while challenging the naturalist explanations or atheist refutations. Part three documents the many instances of mercy bestowed upon repentant sinners. The design of the book is to prove the omniscience, omnipotence, and forgiveness of our God.

www.ingramcontent.com/pod-product-compliance
Lightning Source LLC
Chambersburg PA
CBHW050122020526
44112CB00035B/2343